THE NEW GREAT DEPRESSION

THE NEW

GREAT DEPRESSION

WINNERS AND LOSERS IN
A POST-PANDEMIC WORLD

JAMES RICKARDS

PORTFOLIO / PENGUIN

Portfolio/Penguin
An imprint of Penguin Random House LLC
penguinrandomhouse.com

Most Portfolio books are available at a discount when purchased in quantity for sales
promotions or corporate use. Special editions, which include personalized covers, excerpts,
and corporate imprints, can be created when purchased in large quantities. For more information,
please call (212) 572-2232 or e-mail specialmarkets@penguinrandomhouse.com. Your local
bookstore can also assist with discounted bulk purchases using the Penguin Random House
corporate Business-to-Business program. For assistance in locating a participating retailer,
e-mail B2B@penguinrandomhouse.com.

Library of Congress Control Number: 2020942696

ISBN 9780593330272 (hardcover)
ISBN 9780593330289 (ebook)

Printed in the United States of America
3   5   7   9   10   8   6   4   2

Book design by Daniel Lagin

For those who suffered from the new virus,
and those still suffering and their families.
And for those suffering from the New Great Depression.

And to the memory of Sara Lesley—still standing tall.

And I saw another sign in heaven, great and marvelous, seven angels having the seven last plagues; for in them is filled up the wrath of God.

Revelation 15:1

CONTENTS

INTRODUCTION

Historically, pandemics have forced humans to break with the past and imagine their world anew. This one is no different. It is a portal, a gateway between one world and the next.

—Arundhati Roy, *Financial Times* (April 3, 2020)

It is going to be hard to go back to normal, especially now that we are constantly informed that we cannot go back to normal.

—Lionel Shriver, Spiked (May 11, 2020)

This book is about a virus that caused a global depression. More precisely, it's about how our *reaction* to a virus caused a global depression. A virus can cause disease and pandemic, yet it cannot directly cause an economic collapse; that's up to us.

We made many choices when the extent of the viral attack became clear. Those choices were informed and at times misinformed by science and economics. Since the virus was new and scientists were not in accord, choices offered by science were both muddled and contradictory.

To say the economic choices were muddled and contradictory seems redundant. Still, scientists and economists acted mostly in good faith and always under extreme duress due to the suddenness and lethality of the disease. They did the best they could. It's not clear another expert team would have done better under the circumstances.

As always in crises, there were heroes. Nurses, doctors, and hospital staff were overwhelmed with new cases of infection and coped with acute shortages of protective gear, treatment equipment, and some simple medications. Many worked to the point of exhaustion. Some were infected and, sadly, some died. Individuals attended to loved ones suffering from the virus when hospital facilities were unavailable or unavailing. Sanitation staff scrubbed streets and buildings inside and out to dispel the virus. Charitable groups offered meals to those quarantined or otherwise shut in. Religious bodies erected tent hospitals in bare fields. The Army Corps of Engineers, National Guard, and other military units also built field hospitals almost overnight in large public spaces such as the Javits Center in New York City. Customs and Border Protection officers acted as medical screeners for inbound travelers. The U.S. Navy surged two hospital ships, USNS *Mercy* to Los Angeles and USNS *Comfort* to New York City, to provide added intensive care and surgical capacity to overstretched systems. Similar efforts were made around the world, especially in hard-hit countries like Italy, Spain, Brazil, and the UK. There are more unsung heroes. They all deserve our thanks and prayers.

Still, the suffering of virus victims and the caregivers' sacrifice should not blind us to a different source of misery—the New Great Depression. Policy choices in the face of pandemic have caused the greatest economic collapse in U.S. history. And that collapse is not confined to the United States. The pandemic began in China. It afflicted the greatest number of individuals in the United States, if Chinese data can be believed, which is doubtful. The United States and China are the world's two largest economies, producing 40 percent of global GDP. If the European Union (EU)—home to Italy, France, Spain, and Germany, among other large economies, which have suffered over 130,000 virus-related deaths—is treated as a single economy and added to the United States and China, the percentage of global output subject to pandemic shutdown exceeds 60 percent.

Comparisons to the 2008 global financial crisis, the 2000 dot-com collapse, and the 1998 financial panic miss the point. Those crises, while critical to those affected, were trivial compared with what's upon us now. The first Great Depression, from 1929 to 1940, offers a better frame of reference, yet even that cataclysm does not capture the extent of what happened in 2020 and what is yet to come. The 89.2 percent stock market crash that occurred during the Great Depression played out in stages over four years (1929–32). The 60 million U.S. job losses in the New Great Depression have played out in just over four *months*, and more losses are coming.

This book is written from the perspective of economics, not virology. Still, the topics are intertwined. Writing a book on the New Great Depression without discussing the virus (SARS-CoV-2) would be like writing about destruction and loss of life in New Orleans in 2005 without mentioning Hurricane Katrina. The virus is the hurricane. The depression is the destruction in its wake. We cover both to tell the whole story.

What is a virus? Scientists are not sure. They know a lot *about* viruses. Still, after a century of stunning scientific progress, medicine remains divided on what a virus is. As described by author John M. Barry in his book *The Great Influenza*, viruses are enigmatic:

> Viruses do not eat or burn oxygen for energy. They do not engage
> in any process that could be considered metabolic. They do not

produce waste. They do not have sex. They make no side products, by accident or design. They do not even reproduce independently. They are less than a fully living organism but more than an inert collection of chemicals.

Importantly, scientists are not sure if a virus is even a life form. Some take the view that a virus is a primitive life form from which other more complex forms of life evolved. Others believe that a virus is the result of *devolution* rather than evolution—that the virus had a predecessor, which was a higher form of life that simplified or devolved into what we see today. Another view is that viruses began as part of a living cell that separated and emerged with unique properties, yet not fully alive. Not knowing if a virus is even alive is just the beginning of humankind's struggle with the microscopic foe.

What is known is that a virus is a master of replication. They do not do this on their own. Instead, viruses invade a living cell, take over the host cell's energy and DNA, embed their own genes (coded in RNA, a less complicated form of DNA), and then, in effect, order the host cell to replicate the virus by the thousands. In time, the cell wall bursts, the virus copies are released, and the process continues, now on a far larger scale. A viral swarm has begun.

A virus is no more than an egg-shaped sheath with genetic code inside. The key to replication is what's on the surface of the sheath. The influenza virus has two types of protuberance. The first is a spear made of hemagglutinin ("H"). The second is shaped like a prickly shrub and made of neuraminidase ("N"). The hemagglutinin spears bind to the target cell, "like grappling hooks thrown by pirates onto a vessel," in Barry's words, and begin the genetic invasion. The neuraminidase acts like a battering ram that breaks down sialic acid on the target cell's surface. When the replicated viruses burst from the target cell, they would normally stick to the acid coating. Due to neuraminidase, the coating is destroyed and the new viruses are free to attack other healthy cells.

The H and N abbreviations are familiar to even casual observers of influenza outbreaks. Scientists have identified eighteen elemental shapes for hemagglutinin and nine for neuraminidase. The 1918 Spanish flu was type H1N1. The 1968 Hong Kong flu was type H3N2, still in circulation today. The precise HN structure of SARS-CoV-2 is unknown and is the object of intense research about the structure and behavior of the virus. This research is hampered by apparent rapid mutation of the virus even at this early stage of the pandemic.

What is a depression? Economists have no easier time answering that question than scientists who are asked if a virus is alive. At least scientists are still trying. Economists have given up on the idea of "depressions" and have banned the word from their lexicon. Such behavior is typical of economists, who bury their heads in the sand when facing a real-world problem. Still, depressions do exist; we're in one now. And like viruses, they morph and evolve, ready to attack healthy economies the way a virus attacks a healthy cell. Both pandemics and depressions are rare. Finding economists with a working knowledge of depression dynamics is a singular challenge. The effects of depression can be devastating, even fatal. Just as scientists search for vaccines, economists search for policy solutions to remedy high unemployment, lost output, and collapsing world trade. Scientists don't have all the answers at first, yet they have sound methods for finding answers. Economists don't. That's why the New Great Depression will last longer than the pandemic and have more persistent adverse effects.

Economists are comfortable with the term "recession." A recession is widely understood as two consecutive quarters of declining GDP with rising unemployment. The formal definition as applied by the National Bureau of Economic Research (NBER), the arbiter of recession and recovery, is slightly more complicated, but "two down quarters" is a good rule of thumb. Economists endorse the NBER definition of a recession because it's objective and quantifiable and therefore can be plugged into equations.

Depression fails these objective tests. It's more vaguely defined. It has a powerful psychological element that defies quantification. A depression does not fit easily into equations. Depressions are rare, so they don't play a role in most time series of data used in the regressions and correlations that are the lifeblood of Wall Street's brand of pseudoeconomics.

Even those who use the term "depression" often misconstrue the meaning. Many assume that if a recession means two consecutive quarters of declining GDP, a depression must involve perhaps five or more quarters of decline—in other words, a depression is just a long recession. That's not correct. The first Great Depression, beginning in 1929, included two technical recessions. The first recession ran from August 1929 to March 1933, during which period GDP declined 26.7 percent. The second recession ran from May 1937 to June 1938, during which period GDP declined 18.2 percent. The period 1933–36 was one of strong growth. Stocks rallied 63.7 percent in 1933, 5.4 percent in 1934, 38.5 percent in 1935, and 24.8 percent in 1936 before the second recession hit in 1937; stocks then fell 32.8 percent. Still, the entire period 1929–40 is properly characterized as the Great Depression. The growth from 1933 to 1936 was not enough to undo the stock market decline from 1929 to 1932. In fact, stocks did not regain their 1929 highs until 1954, a full twenty-five years later. Unemployment declined from its peak of 24.9 percent in 1933 yet remained above 14 percent until 1941. Put differently, the economy improved after 1933 but had reached such low levels of employment, output, and stock prices that a badly depressed economy persisted even after improvement began.

A similar pattern prevailed from 1873 to 1897, a period economic historians call the Long Depression. That twenty-four-year depression included six distinct technical recessions of varying lengths and three financial panics (1873, 1893, and 1896). Between these periods of declining output and financial collapse, there was significant real growth and enormous technical innovation. The Long Depression was punctuated by financial failures, including Jay Cooke & Company, the first U.S. investment bank, which financed the Union in the Civil War. The reason this period is called the Long Depression is not primarily due to output declines but rather because of persistent deflation, which burdened business and agriculture by increasing the real value of debt, a topic we explore in chapter 4. If twenty-four years seems like a long depression, give a thought to Japan, which has experienced an ongoing thirty-year depression beginning in 1990.

This brings us to the real meaning of "depression." It does not mean continuous declining output. It means depressed growth relative to trend growth. If an economy is capable of 3 percent growth yet grows for an extended period at 2 percent, it's experiencing depressed growth. Growth can occur during a depression, just as output declines can happen during an expansion. The key lies not in quarterly performance but in the long-term trend relative to potential.

John Maynard Keynes offered the best definition of depression: "a chronic condition of sub-normal activity for a considerable period without any marked tendency either towards recovery or towards complete collapse."

Based on history and Keynes's practical definition, we are now in a new depression that is more far-reaching than a mere technical recession. Depressions are as much psychological as numeric. Output and employment figures matter, but behavioral changes matter more. As growth returns, gains will start from such a depressed plane that the prepandemic output level will not be achieved for years. Unemployment will start to decline, yet from such high levels that hard times will persist for millions of workers for years to come. Numbers aside, behavioral changes will be profound and intergenerational. People will spend less and save more despite White House hectoring to borrow and spend "like the good old days." Those days are over.

Viruses are enigmatic yet well-studied by science, while depressions are real yet ignored by economists. In this book, we explore how the viral enigma emerged and how our response caused a global depression. We cannot blame the virus for the depression; we can only blame ourselves for our response to the virus. That response was the depression's real cause. The consequences will linger long after the virus is contained.

A word on science. Some epidemiologists and immunologists complain that economic analysts should keep out of medicine. The science of viruses, influenza, vaccines, and pandemics is highly technical, takes years of specialized training to master, and requires clinical and laboratory experience to practice expertly. Of course.

Yet immunologists such as Dr. Anthony Fauci, an adviser to President Trump, showed no such restraint when it came to the practice of economic public policy. They claimed that they only made evidence-based recommendations and left economic policy to others. That's untrue. When immunologists demanded the world's largest economy be locked down to mitigate the spread of the SARS-CoV-2 virus, they were implementing the most profound economic policy change in history. You can't have it both ways. Immunologists cannot fundamentally alter the U.S. and global economies, perhaps for decades, while insisting that economic policy makers keep out of immunology.

In the fullness of time, the 2020 lockdown of the U.S. economy will be viewed as the greatest policy blunder ever. Lost wealth and income will be measured in trillions of dollars. Any gain in lives saved or damage avoided was inapposite, since equally effective policy choices were available but untried. There's no evidence that epidemiologists considered lives lost to drugs, alcohol, suicide, and despair when they pursued policies that pushed 60 million Americans out of jobs.

From 1968 to 1969, the H3N2 strain of influenza A virus ravaged the world. Known then as the Hong Kong flu, it killed over 1 million people worldwide and over 100,000 Americans. It was the third-worst influenza pandemic on record, surpassed in fatalities only by the Asian flu (1957–58) and the Spanish flu (1918–20). Prominent fatalities included former CIA director Allen Dulles and Hollywood legend Tallulah Bankhead. President Lyndon Johnson was infected with the flu and survived. An Apollo astronaut, Frank Borman, became ill with the flu in outer space. It was a fierce pandemic with a tragic loss of life, *yet there was no lockdown*. Life in America continued as before. Scientists worked on a vaccine (which was finalized in August 1969), and the public relied on the scientists. Otherwise, life went on. Woodstock occurred during this pandemic. There was no social distancing at Woodstock.

This is not to say mitigation measures should not be used today. They should. Still, immunologists who want to shut down a $22 trillion economy should expect to hear from analysts who take a different view. I've read scores of peer-reviewed papers on epidemiology and economics as research for this book. Both fields are accessible to the educated layperson willing to make the effort to understand the science. I'm not an epidemiologist, but I'm not intimidated by science either. Perhaps two degrees from Johns Hopkins University immunized me from academic angst where natural science is concerned. Of course, I'm perfectly at home in the worlds of public policy and economic analysis.

Chapter 1 explores the best science on the origin of the SARS-CoV-2 virus and the COVID-19 pandemic. Chapter 2 limns the cost and chaos of the global economic lockdown. Chapter 3 describes the New Great Depression in detail both from a quantitative perspective and the perspective of individuals caught in the downdraft. A recovery has begun but will be long, slow, and hard on the lower-paid Americans most affected. Chapter 4 explains why $3 trillion of new Federal Reserve money and $4 trillion of deficit spending by Congress will not cure the depression. Money printing and big spending may help keep the lights on in the economy, but those policies should not be confused with "stimulus." The United States is past the point where stimulus is even possible, except for one little-known policy. Chapter 5 shows that neither pandemic nor economic depression is the worst outcome we can expect. Social disorder around every corner reveals itself daily. The veneer of civilization is paper thin, and the paper is now torn. Chapter 6 offers investors concrete investment strategies to prosper in a postpandemic world. Then the conclusion describes the one economic policy that can rescue the economy. This policy is not understood by politicians and is disdained by economists. Still, it was used by two presidents in the twentieth century and worked well on both occasions. If policy makers won't use this plan to save the economy, you can use it yourself to preserve wealth and prosper in a postpandemic world. Hopefully, this plan gains the support it deserves, so that both the economy and your portfolio will thrive.

Let's begin our tour of this ravaged landscape and, in the end, find our way to a better place.

THE NEW GREAT DEPRESSION

CHAPTER ONE

A NEW VIRUS—FROM CHINA TO A TOWN NEAR YOU

All real scientists exist on the frontier. Even the least ambitious among them deal with the unknown, if only one step beyond the known. The best among them move deep into a wilderness where they know almost nothing.

—John M. Barry, *The Great Influenza* (2005)

The world is waiting for a Wuhan-born virus to run its course. That may never happen.

The virus may grow less lethal by normal mutation. Populations may gain group immunity through exposure to the virus and the passage of time. New treatments and therapies may mitigate the worst outcomes and save lives. Still, a vaccine, while not impossible, may be far off. None of the six known human coronaviruses has ever yielded to immunization by vaccine. The miracle drugs you hear about in the media can immunize against other diseases, such as influenza, that opportunistically attack patients weakened by the virus. Other drugs in development may treat complications from infection by the virus, ease suffering, and save lives. These drugs are valuable and will help the world to cope with the virus. Yet they are not cures. There may never be a cure, just a modus vivendi with an invisible assailant.

The virus is SARS-CoV-2, known popularly as coronavirus. The disease caused by the virus is COVID-19. The disease itself is a mystery. It can present as little more than a common cold, with coughing, slight fever, a headache, and a runny nose. In some cases, infection presents no symptoms at all; it just comes and goes through a victim with no sign it was ever there except an invisible trail of antibodies that might be detected with a subsequent test.

Yet in some cases the virus presents in violent and potentially fatal form. Patients have trouble breathing, the result of lung inflammation. Minute air sacs in the lungs fill with liquid that can make it impossible for the lungs to transfer oxygen to the blood. In effect, the victim is drowning in his own bodily fluids, a condition called pulmonary edema. Some patients report intense pain in the lungs and describe it like swallowing broken glass. High fevers hit victims hard.

From there, complications multiply rapidly. Once oxygen intake slows, organ failure follows. Victims can experience kidney failure, heart attacks, blood clots, high blood pressure, or sepsis, a type of blood poisoning. With the patient in vulnerable condition, other infections arise as different viruses and bacteria attack opportunistically. This results in influenza and both bacterial and viral pneumonia. Some of these complications can be treated individually. Still, there is no single cure.

In the worst cases, complications strike almost any organ or bodily system for reasons medicine does not understand. Some victims experience brain damage and nervous-system failures resulting in cognitive dysfunction or hallucinations. A loss of the senses of smell and taste is common. Strokes and intestinal inflammation are also reported. The high fevers, acute respiratory distress, and multiple infections, and the speed with which these converge, result in death in a significant percentage of acute cases.

In the resulting deluge of information, some expert, some reckless, it's important to be clear on two points. COVID-19 is not influenza, and it is not pneumonia. Those are separate diseases that can strike COVID-19 victims. They can be fatal, especially in conjunction with other COVID-19 complications. COVID-19 itself is a strange new disease. In its pure form and without complications, the disease presents somewhat like acute mountain sickness, a disease I've suffered myself in high-altitude mountaineering. For the mountaineer, the best cure is rapid descent, although in extreme cases a portable hyperbaric chamber (called a Gamow Bag) or a helicopter rescue is needed. It's just a matter of getting more oxygen fast. For the COVID-19 victim, pure oxygen administered with a cannula or face mask is one of the most effective treatments.

This pure oxygen therapy was used for UK prime minister Boris Johnson during his acute COVID-19 attack, which stretched over two weeks in early April 2020. Johnson told reporters, "It was hard to believe that in just a few days my health had deteriorated to this extent." Johnson's doctors made the right choice. The alternative was use of a ventilator and a medically induced coma. The evidence is now strong that overuse of ventilators did more harm than good in COVID-19 cases and caused death in many cases. Most patients don't need a mechanical lung. They need oxygen.

The mystery of COVID-19 was captured by the *Wall Street Journal*, which focused on the unusual array of complications presented by patients and the reaction of seasoned professionals to a totally new disease:

> The virus's strange effects go beyond anything doctors say they usually see with other viral infections. "It seems to strike so many systems," said Maya Rao, a nephrologist . . . in New York

who is treating Covid-19 patients with acute kidney failure. "We don't understand who gets it." . . .

"Sometimes with very severe infections you can see things similar to this," said Magdy Selim, a neurologist . . . in Boston, who is treating Covid-19 patients who have had strokes. "But not all this combination of things in one patient. These are really sick patients."

In just a few months from December 2019 to March 2020, COVID-19 went from a regional epidemic to a global pandemic. By early October 2020, global fatalities exceeded one million and were rising steadily.

Before turning to the pandemic's economic impact, this book's main topic, it's critical to trace the origin and spread of the SARS-CoV-2 virus. This is as much a mystery as a medical inquiry. Fortunately, there are abundant clues. The viral spread has geopolitical implications that rival such epochal events as the end of the Cold War in 1991 and the Great Depression of 1929–40. It's impossible to comprehend the social consequences of the virus without grasping the viral spread itself.

China's negligence (or worse) caused a local outbreak to become a pandemic. America suffered the most and paid the highest price in lives and lost wealth. Today all countries are consumed with containing the virus or cleaning up the economic rubble or both. Yet there is unfinished business between the world's two economic superpowers, the United States and China, in terms of responsibility for the pandemic.

In H. G. Wells's classic 1898 science fiction novel *The War of the Worlds*, Martians invade Earth and wreak havoc with Heat Rays and fighting machines. The Martians are merciless, killing humans on sight while capturing some to remove their blood for Martian nourishment. In the end, the Martians are defeated—not by the armies of mankind but by a bacterium to which Martians have no immunity. In Wells's story, a mysterious microbe brings peace and saves humanity.

Now the opposite is true. A mysterious virus has brought death and may ultimately bring war as relations between China and the United States decline due to a damaged and demoralized U.S. economy. To solve this viral mystery, we begin with the path of the virus, then turn to paths the world economy may take in its wake.

FROM WUHAN TO THE WORLD

The pandemic began in Wuhan, a city of eleven million people in Hubei Province in central China, halfway between Shanghai and Chongqing. Wuhan lies along the Yangtze River, the longest river in Asia and most important waterway in China, which flows from the Tibetan Plateau to Shanghai on the East China Sea. The Yangtze is at the heart of Han Chinese culture, and Wuhan has played a pivotal role in that culture for millennia.

Americans who have been to Wuhan are generally either business travelers or those disembarking from a Three Gorges river expedition. The Three Gorges are a narrow section of the Yangtze that form a steep canyon with tricky currents. The vistas are spectacular, yet not quite as impressive as they were before the opening of the Three Gorges Dam west of Wuhan. The dam raised the river's water level three hundred feet in the gorges, inundating historical sites in the process. I visited Wuhan in 1993 expressly to view the Three Gorges in prediluvian form. I journeyed upriver to Chongqing instead of the usual downriver trip because the boat went against the river's flow, allowing more time to appreciate the experience. Before embarking from Wuhan, I dodged the awful food on my vessel and wandered down the city's alleys in search of the best street-vendor dumplings. I found them prepared by an old woman, served straight from the wok with Chinese chilis on the side. I didn't ask what was inside the dumplings. I would not repeat the romp today.

While traditional manufacturing continues in Wuhan, the city has also led the way in technology, with over 350 research centers and thousands of high-tech firms. Among these centers are three high-level bio-research facilities, including the biosafety-level-four Wuhan Institute of Virology. Since January 2020, the Wuhan Institute has effectively been overseen by People's Liberation Army major general Chen Wei, who is China's top military microbiologist.

The first officially documented COVID-19 case is now dated to November 17, 2019, according to Chinese government data as reported by the *South China Morning Post*. The patient was a fifty-five-year old resident of Hubei Province living near Wuhan. This person is not necessarily Patient Zero; finding that individual requires contact tracing of the November 17 case. There is some evidence that cases arose before November 17; that inquiry is still under way.

From there, the disease spread to 9 confirmed cases—four men and five women—in November and 266 confirmed cases by December 31, 2019. Epidemics spread exponentially. They begin with a few cases, grow slowly, and then suddenly explode as the exponential function takes control. This was the case with COVID-19.

Total confirmed cases in China were still fewer than 10,000 by the end of January 2020. That figure approached 80,000 by the end of February. By then, this was no longer just China's epidemic. Over 5,000 additional cases were reported outside China, with over 1,000 of those cases in Italy alone. The transition from epidemic to pandemic had begun.

As explosive as the growth of new cases in China was, it is almost certainly an undercount and an official deception. The real spread in Wuhan and China was far worse. A study by the American Enterprise

Institute using reliable travel data and reasonable assumptions on the infection rate estimates the number of COVID-19 cases in China at 2.9 million. Perhaps 200,000 Chinese died. Ample anecdotal and empirical evidence supports these estimates.

Eyewitness accounts report that in a two-week period from March 23 to April 4, 2020, over five hundred urns of victim ashes were delivered to families in Wuhan every day. That data suggests 7,000 dead in Wuhan alone in a fairly brief period, compared with China's official report of just over 4,700 dead in the entire country from November 2019 to October 2020. Both eyewitnesses and U.S. intelligence sources report that incinerators in Wuhan were in use twenty-four hours a day in March and April and as many as 45,500 corpses may have been cremated. The truth may never be known, because China has no interest in revealing the truth and every interest in hiding it from the world.

What is clear is that millions traveled from Wuhan during the critical stages in January and February, and hundreds of thousands traveled from Beijing and Shanghai to cities around the world. China was exporting the virus. While early cases began appearing in Seattle, the next global hot spot to emerge was Italy.

The Italian outbreak was carried by Chinese citizens arriving in Milan for Fashion Week, which ran from February 18 through February 24, 2020. These Chinese were not only active participants in Fashion Week but also own a substantial part of the Italian fashion industry, based in northern Italy. There were only 62 confirmed cases in Italy as of February 22, near the end of Fashion Week. Given the one- to two-week period during which the infected are asymptomatic, one would have expected the reported caseload to explode around March 1. That's exactly what happened. Italian confirmed cases went from 1,694 on March 1 to 7,375 on March 8 to 24,747 on March 15 to 59,138 on March 22. The caseload was more than doubling, sometimes tripling every week. By early October there were more than 300,000 confirmed cases in Italy. The country's fatalities kept pace, with over 35,000 dead, the sixth-highest national fatality count in the world after the United States, Brazil, Mexico, India, and the UK.

The Italian tragedy was amplified by an older demographic and strained health-care facilities. Italy (like other countries) was slow to respond to the pandemic at first but then moved dramatically with a regional and then national lockdown. The country was able to "flatten the curve" of newly infected by April 1, at which time the new-case count dropped below five thousand per day. By early May, the rate of new cases was below two thousand per day. By June 1, the rate fell to one thousand per day. In a nation of over sixty million people, this represented a huge success. Yet success at controlling the outbreak came after incalculable costs in terms of lives lost and human suffering.

Italy was a warning to the rest of the world in part because earlier Chinese data was fabricated and could not be relied upon by policy makers as a guide. In contrast, Italian data was reliable and told a horrifying story of contagion and exponential spread. This was why other developed economies were late in implementing protective measures. Chinese data, although flawed, suggested containment was possible. The Italian data showed the epidemic was not contained in China and would spread explosively in other high-density environments. It was the unfolding disaster in Italy that finally put the United States and Europe on high alert. Still, it was too late. By early March, the virus had gone global and the explosion in caseloads hit Spain, France, Germany, and the United States in rapid succession. March 15, 2020, marks the date when the global caseload chart went vertical, forming a classic "hockey stick" shape. On March 15, the global caseload was 167,000. By March 31, just over two weeks later, the figure was 858,000. By October 1, 2020, there were over 32 million confirmed cases. Individual cities and countries were trying to flatten their curves. The global curve had not flattened at all.

What is the course of the virus from here? It's a mystery; scientists are still coming to grips with the SARS-CoV-2 virus and the COVID-19 disease. The genome is known, but the viral composition in terms of HN structures and other properties is still under study. Even the published genome does not capture all of the mutations that are occurring rapidly.

The behavior of the virus and how COVID-19 presents in patients are also not well understood. SARS-CoV-2 is a type of coronavirus, and coronaviruses are quite different from influenza viruses. Still, the two types of viruses have traits in common. There is enormous benefit in studying past pandemics as a way to unravel the mystery of COVID-19.

There have been eight major influenza pandemics since the 1700s. Of these, four emerged since 1900: the Spanish flu (1918–19), the Asian flu (1957), the Hong Kong flu (1968), and the swine flu (2009). The course of those pandemics and their similarities to COVID-19 are instructive.

These four influenza viruses and SARS-CoV-2 were all new viruses to which the human population had scant immunity. While not everyone would be infected or severely impacted, the entire world population was potentially susceptible. Both SARS-CoV-2 and the influenza viruses are highly contagious and move rapidly. This meant the viruses could spread globally before mitigation measures such as quarantine were put in place. All of these viruses spread to victims' respiratory systems through large droplets and small airborne particles as a result of sneezing, coughing, or even normal breathing by carriers. Other transmission methods, including carriers touching objects such as doorknobs that are later touched by victims, are also possible.

Differences existed between SARS-CoV-2 and the influenza viruses that made the former more contagious and potentially more lethal. The incubation period during which an infected party could spread the disease without exhibiting symptoms is in the range of two to four days for influenza and two to fourteen days for SARS-CoV-2. This expanded incubation period means that SARS-CoV-2 can spread further before authorities are alerted and precautions can be taken in a specific locality. As pointed out in late April 2020 by the Center for Infectious Disease Research and Policy (CIDRAP), this longer incubation period also meant that governments might remain complacent at a time when rigorous mitigation measures should have been deployed.

Another factor increasing the likelihood of infectious spread for COVID-19 is the ease with which is virus is transmitted. Viral transmissibility is measured by a reproductive number (R0), which is the average number of new infections from one infected person, assuming the entire population is susceptible to infection. Where R0 is greater than 1, each infected person is giving the disease to more than one person and the disease is spreading exponentially. Where R0 is less than 1, each infected person is spreading the disease to less than one other person; the pandemic is dying out.

The R0 for the SARS-CoV-2 virus in China was estimated at 2.0 to 2.5 by a study published in the medical journal *The Lancet*, while other studies suggest the factor may be higher, depending on population density of affected groups and the role of so-called superspreaders. In contrast, major influenza pandemics of the past hundred years had an R0 value of less than 2.

Taking into account the incubation period, the size of the asymptomatic population, transmissibility (R0), and other factors, it appears that SARS-CoV-2 spreads more rapidly and persistently than the viruses responsible for the worst influenza pandemics since 1900. This alone does not make the SARS-CoV-2 virus more lethal than earlier influenza viruses. The H1N1 influenza virus of the 1918 Spanish flu killed over 100 million people, by some estimates. It does mean that SARS-CoV-2 may be more robust and last longer in human populations than influenza viruses. It also leaves open the possibility that a second wave of infections may arrive in 2021 and be even more lethal than the first wave of December 2019–October 2020.

Based on the pattern of the four influenza pandemics noted and the similarities between the viruses that caused them and SARS-CoV-2, the following three scenarios for COVID-19 are among the most likely patterns to expect in the months ahead.

Scenario 1 involves a series of waves of increasing infections followed by decreasing infections followed by another increase. The good news is that each wave would be slightly smaller than the one before (due to growing herd immunity) as the virus slowly disappears (in part because of a diminishing pool of susceptible targets). The bad news is this pattern might persist until late 2021 or early 2022. In effect, we would learn to live with COVID-19 even as mitigation strategies were dialed up and dialed back down with each wave.

Scenario 2 also involves repetitive waves. The difference is that the second wave (arriving in 2021) would be far more lethal than the first wave of 2020, due possibly to a mutation or recombination of genetic material. This pattern was seen in the 1918 Spanish flu, the 1957 Asian flu, and the 2009 swine flu. In all three pandemics, a moderate yet lethal wave began in the spring and subsided by the early summer. Then, in the fall, a larger, superlethal wave of infections arrived.

Scenario 3 is the most optimistic case. In this scenario, the worst is already behind us. There will be more waves, but they will be progressively smaller even to the point of not constituting a true wave, just a slight increase in infections compared with the prior month or quarter. The modelers at CIDRAP refer to this pattern as a "slow burn."

Regardless of the pattern that emerges, all three scenarios can be mitigated by commonsense solutions such as social distancing, face masks, frequent hand washing, limiting crowd sizes, and voluntary self-quarantine by those most vulnerable, including those over sixty-five years old and those with respiratory problems, diabetes, or compromised immune systems. Neither scenario 1 nor scenario 3 would require extreme lockdown measures of the kind the U.S. economy (and economies abroad) have experienced over the course of March–October 2020.

The danger is that we experience scenario 2, in which our struggle in the first half of 2020 is just a glimpse of a greater horror to come. In that case, the return of extreme lockdown measures of the kind that were recently lifted should be expected.

Unfortunately, the fact that three of the four great influenza pandemics since 1918 have followed the scenario 2 second-wave pattern, and similarities between COVID-19 and these influenza pandemics in general, leaves open the specter of a larger, more lethal wave to come. The quiet period between waves varies from four to six months. As the first wave abates in October 2020, this suggests the second wave may hit around April 2021. The early-winter months in the Northern Hemisphere coincide with what is normally peak season for other influenza strains. While COVID-19 is not influenza, its effects can weaken the body's immune system to the point where separate influenza viruses and forms of pneumonia invade the victim's body on their own and cause extensive damage, even death. One hopes this scenario does not play out. Still, a second wave is a real possibility, and it is far too soon to dismiss it out of hand.

Insofar as infection waves are concerned, COVID-19 appears to run its course from outbreak to peak to diminished impact in eight to ten weeks without regard to the extent of mitigation. This fits the pattern seen in New York City, by far the highest-fatality site in the United States with over 23,000 deaths as of October 1, 2020, over 11 percent of the total COVID-19 deaths in the United States. The daily fatality rate in New York City began to rise rapidly in early March 2020, reached a peak in mid-April, and then substantially subsided by mid-May. This fits the eight-to-ten-week outbreak pattern almost perfectly. There is strong statistical evidence from case studies to support this hypothesis.

That said, this eight-to-ten-week wave duration, if valid, applies to each wave. Any second or third waves would presumably have their own eight-to-ten-week terms. In assessing global prospects, it's also critical to know that each wave runs its course in a locality (which can be a large area such as the northeastern United States or the entire UK), but not all localities' waves emerge at the same time. Obviously, Wuhan was the first outbreak, yet it was mostly contained by the time an intense outbreak covered most of New York City and surrounding parts of New Jersey. Russia had a relatively late outbreak that was escalating rapidly even as New York was subsiding. Each of these waves may have an eight-to-ten-week term, yet they do not necessarily run concurrently; they run sequentially, depending on the appearance of Patient Zero. This adds to the mystery; late first waves are mistaken for global second waves.

By late May, the sense of relief in New York City hospitals and emergency rooms was palpable. The pandemic was not over; patients were still dying. Yet the tempo had dropped off considerably. If not quite normal, the hospital workers felt that some sense of normality was returning after the onslaught of sick and dying patients and the overcrowding they had confronted in April.

Still, relief at the reduction in new cases was tempered by a sense of dread that another wave might be coming. The *New York Times* reported on this mixture of relief and apprehension:

> "It's almost this eerie silence," said Dr. Sylvie de Souza, chair of the emergency department at the Brooklyn Hospital Center, an independent institution where the daily E.R. volume last week was less than half of the 200 to 250 patients it typically saw before the pandemic. "None of us are at peace. We're sort of bracing for

it to come back. All of us are wondering, can we go through this again?"

One's view of the pandemic's progress depended on one's location. In New York, it seemed the worst was over by May. In other states and cities, the numbers of confirmed infections and fatalities were rising at an accelerated tempo. Michigan, Pennsylvania, and Illinois were all hard hit after a somewhat slow start to the spread in March and April. Likewise, Texas and California saw spikes in cases after being applauded for earlier success at containing the virus. California reported over 790,000 confirmed cases as of October 1, 2020, after reporting fewer than 53,000 cases on May 1, 2020.

Globally, the situation was growing worse. Total new cases reported worldwide were 98,800 on April 12; 100,200 on May 15; and 324,200 on September 18, 2020. There were peaks and valleys in the daily case figures, yet the trend was unmistakable and ominous. The disease was still spreading; the data was still getting worse. Countries of particular concern included Russia, where the daily new case count went from 501 on March 31, 2020, to 11,700 on May 11. By early October there were over 1,110,000 confirmed cases in Russia (compared with over 6,875,000 in the United States). Countries including the UK, Italy, and Spain had already suffered mightily, with high fatalities in March and April. Brazil had over 137,000 dead. Mexico, India, and Iran joined the ranks of those with fatalities between 25,000 and 90,000 each.

While those locked down waited for good news, the news got worse and the mystery surrounding the virus deepened. A scientific study released on June 12, 2020, showed that a mutation in the virus, called by some the Italian strain based on the likely site of the mutation, increased the ability of the virus to infect new victims through changes in the spike protein that facilitates the viral invasion of healthy cells. This mutation, known as the G variant (in contrast to a forerunner D amino acid), has displaced the original viral genome worldwide. Northwestern University virologist Judd Hultquist said, "We were unable to deal with D. If G transmits even better, we're going to be unable to deal with that one."

The rise in global infected was relentless. Over thirty-two million confirmed cases and over 1,000,000 deaths were reported worldwide by October 1, 2020. By far the leader in global fatalities was the United States, with over 200,000 dead by early October. Over 53,000 died in New York, New Jersey, and Connecticut alone, over twenty-five percent of the United States total. What started in Wuhan had landed like a viral H-bomb in Times Square and devastated surrounding communities. It was hard to meet anyone in New York who did not know someone who had died or suffered badly in the viral storm.

Going forward, the best case is that we'll see regional peaks in a single-peak pattern, followed by progressively smaller waves until the disease mutates to a manageable form. The worst case is that the October 2020 peak is followed in six months by a second wave of greater virulence, producing more violent deaths on a far greater scale. History and science suggest that the worst case cannot be dismissed; it may be the most likely.

AN UNKNOWN COMPLICATION

The COVID-19 pandemic began in Wuhan in November 2019, possibly earlier. The epidemiological evidence measured in reported cases, fatalities, geographic scope of the outbreak, time line of the spread, and strong anecdotal evidence make that clear.

Did the virus originally spring from a laboratory or a wet market? That question is an enduring mystery of the pandemic with immense implications for U.S.-China relations and, by extension, the global economy.

Responsibility for the initial handling of an outbreak rests with the leadership of the country where the outbreak originates. The best course is to act quickly, report honestly, and invite teams of international scientists to assist in containing the spread and treating the victims. Viral investigators can identify and isolate the pathogen. Research on vaccines and treatments can begin immediately. Every minute counts. This approach invites international team science in the best sense. The United States and other nations and international organizations, including the Red Cross and Red Crescent societies, were ready and willing to assist the victims in China and stop the spread of SARS-CoV-2.

China did not make use of this assistance. Its leaders were at first in denial, both at the provincial government level and within the Communist Party leadership. When they did react, in late December 2019, they took steps to cover up the disease.

Dr. Li Wenliang, a thirty-four-year-old Chinese ophthalmologist at the Wuhan Central Hospital, was among the first to comprehend the extent of the outbreak, in late December. He sent messages to fellow doctors on December 30 about cases that were appearing and the negligent response by local officials. He warned medical personnel to wear surgical gloves and other protective clothing when treating patients.

Instead of commending Li and following his lead, the local Public Security Bureau ordered him to appear in person at its headquarters. Li was told he was under investigation for "spreading rumours." He was accused of "making false comments" and told he had "severely disturbed the social order." Li was ordered to sign a statement that said, in part: "We solemnly warn you: If you keep being stubborn, with such impertinence, and continue this illegal activity, you will be brought to justice—is that understood?"

China should have learned from Li's transparency. Instead it used its state apparatus to suppress the truth. On January 10, 2020, Dr. Li showed signs of the disease, including an intense cough. He had contracted

COVID-19 from an infected glaucoma patient he was treating. On January 13 he entered the hospital with a high fever and other complications. On February 7 he died from the virus. To millions around the world, Li was a hero. To the Communist Party of China, he was a dissident who needed to be silenced.

Communist China's chairman Xi did order Wuhan to take drastic measures on January 7 and locked down the city on January 23. By then it was too late. Millions of travelers had left China since the November 2019 outbreak and spread the disease to Seattle, Milan, and other cities around the world. The Chinese epidemic was now a pandemic. Scientists estimate that 95 percent of global infections would have been prevented if China had not engaged in its cover-up and had reached out to other nations for expert assistance.

China enlisted the help of the UN's World Health Organization (WHO) to implement its cover-up. The WHO is headed by Director-General Tedros Adhanom Ghebreyesus, who was elected in May 2017 with strong political and financial support from Communist China and Tedros's comrades-in-arms from Ethiopia's revolutionary Tigray People's Liberation Front. Tedros repaid his benefactors by spreading lies about the virus using his WHO platform.

On January 14, 2020, WHO issued an official tweet that said, "Preliminary investigations conducted by the Chinese authorities have found no clear evidence of human-to-human transmission of the novel #coronavirus (2019-nCoV) identified in #Wuhan, #China." The tweet was a lie. China had been fighting the disease for months and saw evidence of human-to-human transmission in thousands of cases. There was no evidence to the contrary. The WHO simply parroted the Chinese party line.

On January 30, 2020, the WHO called the outbreak a "public health emergency" but refused to use the word "pandemic," even though the disease had already spread to eighteen countries besides China at the

time. The omission of the word "pandemic" was another WHO deception, since the global spread of the disease had already happened, and the
pandemic's path was clear based on China's own experience. The WHO
was little more than a Chinese propaganda channel.

On April 14, 2020, U.S. president Donald Trump announced the
United States was suspending its WHO funding pending further review.
Trump made this decision based on the "World Health Organization's
role in severely mismanaging and covering up the spread of the coronavirus." On May 29, 2020, Trump followed through on his threat and terminated the U.S. relationship with the WHO; he directed that $400
million in funds previously provided by the United States to the WHO
(15 percent of the WHO's total budget) be redirected to other international health initiatives. Trump said, "Chinese officials ignored their reporting obligations to the World Health Organization and pressured the
World Health Organization to mislead the world." Chinese aid to the
WHO was only $86 million per year. In effect, the United States was
withdrawing from a once-respected organization that had devolved into
a Chinese Communist Party mouthpiece.

The Chinese government cover-up did not end even when the extent
of the pandemic was clear to the world. In February 2020, China ex-
pelled three reporters for the *Wall Street Journal*. In mid-March it ex-
pelled additional journalists from the *Wall Street Journal*, the *New York
Times*, and the *Washington Post*. China did not want seasoned reporters
investigating the origins of the virus.

Why?

China's actions in suppressing the truth, using the WHO to promote
its lies internationally, and expelling independent journalists are all consistent with the actions of someone with something to hide. What was
China hiding?

What China wanted to hide was not the disease itself; that was impossible. China was hiding the *source* of the disease. This was an effort to deflect responsibility and neutralize trillions of dollars of damage claims. China needed to make the viral spread appear natural and unintended. China went further, using its new "wolf warrior" diplomacy, and blamed the United States for releasing the virus. Above all, China's goal was to impede an inquiry into the real source of the virus. As long as there was no international investigation of the true source, China was free to propagate whatever version it liked.

There are two principal theories for the source of the virus at the time of its transfer to humans. The first is the "wet market" theory. The second is the "laboratory" theory. The difference matters greatly for the future of U.S.-China relations. The stakes for global commerce if communication between the world's two largest economies breaks down could not be greater. These two virus-origination theories can be explored with available sources. This is a mystery that can be solved.

Cities and villages throughout China host what are called "wet markets." That term is used to describe an open-air market that offers wildlife for slaughter by market butchers. Popular animals eaten by customers include dogs, bats, civet cats, and pangolins, scale-covered mammals that resemble anteaters and are considered a delicacy. Because the animals are kept caged and are slaughtered on the spot, these markets are filled with blood and feces. Wet markets have been identified as one source of the SARS-CoV virus (found in Himalayan palm civets and racoon dogs), and serological evidence supports the view that this virus transferred from animals to humans (a process called zoonotic transfer) as the result of close contact between humans and animals and the presence of blood.

The science is also clear that bats carry coronaviruses that can sometimes infect humans through zoonotic transfers. Given the evidence that SARS-CoV transferred to humans through civets sold in wet markets, it is not difficult to take the view that SARS-CoV-2, the virus that causes COVID-19, also made the zoonotic transfer from bats to humans through a wet-market slaughter and quick consumption by an unsuspecting customer. This is a preferred Chinese narrative because the viral transfer would have been unintentional—just an unfortunate accident with unfortunate consequences.

The second theory is that the SARS-CoV-2 virus was experimented with in a laboratory in Wuhan and the virus infected a lab worker, who carried the infection outside the lab and infected others.

There are two major laboratories in Wuhan that conduct biological research involving bat coronaviruses that could potentially jump to humans. One is the Wuhan Institute of Virology and the other is Wuhan Center for Disease Control and Prevention. Risky experiments involving genetic engineering using a reverse genetics system on a SARS-like virus existing in Chinese horseshoe bats resulted in an artificial virus (chimeric virus) that could "replicate efficiently in primary human airway cells," according to a scientific paper coauthored by Dr. Shi Zhengli-Li. Dr. Shi is the director of the Center for Emerging Infectious Diseases at the Wuhan Institute of Virology. Such experiments did not necessarily involve biowarfare; they could have been aimed at understanding coronaviruses and developing vaccines. Dr. Shi's work has been heavily criticized by other scientists as involving excessive risk relative to potential benefits. In January 2018, the U.S. embassy in Beijing sent diplomatic cables to Washington, DC, warning that the Wuhan Institute of Virology "has a serious shortage of appropriately trained technicians and investigators needed to safely operate this high-containment laboratory." The Wuhan Institute of Virology had posted a notice on its website about the visits by American scientists sent from the U.S. embassy. That notice was erased from the website by the lab in early April 2020 yet remains available on the internet. On May 24, 2020, the Wuhan Institute of Virology publicly admitted that it has three live strains of bat coronavirus on-site. The lab's director, Wang Yangi, said the lab "isolated and obtained some coronaviruses from bats," and "we have three strains of live viruses." The director went on to say the lab's viruses did not closely resemble SARS-CoV-2. Still, Chinese government statements lack credibility because of their persistent pattern of demonstrable lies about the virus.

In sum, we know the Wuhan Institute of Virology possesses live bat coronaviruses, conducted risky experiments on bat-to-human transmission, and has deficient safety procedures.

The wet-market theory is anecdotal and cannot be proved or disproved without more investigation by virologists. China's government has prohibited investigation by anyone except its own approved scientists. China caused the disappearance of individuals who dissented from the wet-market narrative and erased the social media posts of others. China lied repeatedly about the spread of the disease and the number of cases and fatalities. No investigation produced by Chinese officials alone can be relied on because of this documented pattern of cover-up and deception.

There are serious flaws in the wet-market theory. *Washington Post* columnist David Ignatius pointed out that bats were not sold at the Huanan Seafood Market in Wuhan, the wet market officially identified by the Chinese government as the source of the coronavirus (although the virus could have moved from bats to other animals sold at that wet market). The type of bat that carries the lethal coronavirus is not found within a hundred miles of Wuhan. *The Lancet* published an article on January 24, 2020, that showed 75 percent (three out of four) of the earliest identified cases of COVID-19 in one study involved individuals who had no prior exposure to the Huanan Seafood Market. Gao Fu, the director of China's Centers for Disease Control and Prevention, said that he and his team of inspectors examined the Huanan Seafood Market in early January 2020 and found no coronavirus traces in any animal samples tested.

The laboratory theory has also come under attack. One article claims to show that SARS-CoV-2 could not have been bioengineered in a laboratory because the genetic data for the virus shows no sign of the use of reverse genetic systems that are a hallmark of genetic manipulation. Yet informed parties have not claimed the virus was bioengineered, only that it leaked from a laboratory through negligence. Most virology labs have large numbers of caged animals for experimental purposes. These animals may have had SARS-CoV-2 in a natural form and passed the virus to humans through blood, feces, or contact with other bodily fluids. Saying the virus was not engineered is not the same as saying it did not come from a lab. The widely cited article proves nothing with regard to the source of the virus. The study was partially funded by the Chinese government.

A more recent study (still pending peer review as of this writing) from Flinders University professor Nikolai Petrovsky, a prominent virologist, suggests that SARS-CoV-2 may be the result of a cell-culture experiment in a laboratory. Petrovsky observed that SARS-CoV-2 had genetic elements that resembled bat coronaviruses and other coronaviruses. Petrovsky sees this as possibly the result of a recombination event, in which two viruses naturally swap genetic material *without* the intervention of genetic engineering. This report reconciles the view that SARS-CoV-2 was not bioengineered with the view that it did leak from a laboratory. Petrovsky does not rule out a viral recombination in animals but finds the petri-dish possibility more likely. "It was like it was designed to infect humans," he says.

The issue is far from settled (few topics in science ever are). A paper dated May 28, 2020, accepted for publication in the *Quarterly Review of Biophysics* points to evidence of "inserted sections placed on the SARS-CoV-2 Spike surface," which enhance the potential for infectious and lethal traits in the virus. This means the virus *was* bioengineered in a laboratory. According to one report, the coauthor of the paper, Norwegian scientist Birger Sørensen said that "the virus has properties that differ greatly from SARS . . . and have never been detected in nature," and that both the United States and China had conducted "gain of function" experiments "in which the pathogenicity or transmissibility of potential pandemic pathogens can be enhanced."

The most rigorously researched claim that the virus emerged from the Wuhan Institute laboratory and was bioengineered came from Chinese virologist Dr. Li-Meng Yan of the University of Hong Kong Medical Centre School of Public Health, which includes a reference laboratory for the World Health Organization. Dr. Yan fled from Hong Kong to the United States in April 2020 out of fear for her safety. Detailed scientific evidence for the claims of Dr. Yan and her colleagues was contained in a paper published on September 14, 2020.

There is clear consensus that the COVID-19 outbreak began in Wuhan in late 2019. There is also consensus that the SARS-CoV-2 virus was not bioengineered (with some opposing views). The consensus view is that the virus first existed in animals and infected humans through either zoonotic transfer or a petri dish. There is no consensus on whether that transfer took place by accident in a wet market or by accident in a laboratory, possibly the Wuhan Institute of Virology. There is clear evidence that the Wuhan Institute has live bat coronavirus strains today and has conducted risky experiments involving the possibility of transfer to humans in the past. There is also clear evidence that the earliest cases of COVID-19 in China had *not* visited the Huanan Seafood Market in Wuhan (the government's claimed wet market).

Almost all other evidence on the origin of the virus transfer to humans is circumstantial. Chinese health operatives did bleach the wet market stalls to make it impossible to test for the presence of SARS-CoV-2 in the wet market. Chinese officials did order the destruction of virus samples in the country's genomics labs. Australia's *Daily Telegraph* reported that "the Chinese government deliberately covered up the coronavirus by silencing doctors who spoke out, destroying evidence from the Wuhan laboratory and refusing to provide live virus samples to international scientists working on a vaccine." In mid-January 2020, near the height of the COVID-19 outbreak in China, the Chinese government sent People's Liberation Army major general Chen Wei, a fifty-four-year-old virologist and noted expert in biochemical warfare, to the Wuhan Institute of Virology to direct the outbreak containment effort.

Since suggestions the virus leaked from the Wuhan Institute lab were first publicized, China has engaged in a sophisticated global propaganda campaign that has at various times suggested the virus originated with the U.S. military, demanded the U.S. reveal its own biological research at Fort Detrick in Frederick, Maryland, and ridiculed Secretary of State Mike Pompeo. China's propaganda plan was revealed in an article in *China Daily* titled "Shape Global Narratives for Telling China's Stories." The article states, "A country's ability to get its messages across internationally determines its influence, while its narrative determines its ability to seize the initiative in its global interactions. In international communications theory, the 'narrative' is a communication tool that conveys specific values. . . . To be effective, the narrative needs to be supported by high-quality content. Second is the ability to set the agenda in the international arena." Indeed. If you're telling the truth, you don't need a narrative.

Intelligence analysis almost never proceeds from a complete set of facts. The raw materials usually consist of some facts, some smart suppositions, and reasonable inferences using sophisticated applied mathematical tools, including Bayes' theorem, behavioral science, and complexity theory. If one had all the facts, the job would be easy. It isn't.

The wet-markets theory is a reasonable supposition with few facts to support it and ample facts that call the theory into question. The laboratory theory is also a reasonable supposition with ample facts to support it and no facts that contradict it. To solve this mystery, an intelligence analyst would ask the following:

Why would China destroy evidence if the virus did not come from a laboratory?

Why would China assign a PLA major general and biological warfare expert to the Wuhan Institute if that was not the source of the problem?

What are the probabilities that a laboratory with live strains of bat coronavirus and a poor safety record might accidentally leak a virus lethal to humans?

What are the probabilities that a wet market with no bats for sale and none within a hundred miles would be the source of a bat coronavirus?

What are the probabilities that the wet market in Wuhan was the source of the human coronavirus when three out of four of the first victims had not been to the wet market?

Why would China engage in a sophisticated global propaganda campaign trying to shift blame to the United States if China had nothing to hide?

None of these questions can be answered definitively without access to the highest levels of the Chinese government and on-the-ground inspections in Wuhan. Both access and inspections are denied to independent investigators at the moment. Much pertinent evidence has already been destroyed. Key witnesses were made to disappear.

Still, the questions are framed in a way that answers can be found using available evidence, inference, and conditional probabilities. Conclusions are obtained by multiplying the individual probabilities. Using these methods, the evidence points strongly to a conclusion that the lethal virus leaked from the Wuhan Institute of Virology. We may never know for certain, unless secret Chinese archives are released in the decades to come, perhaps after a regime change.

Independent of whether the virus came from a wet market or a laboratory, China cannot disclaim responsibility for the economic damage caused and lives lost in the resulting global pandemic. Chinese involvement in the cover-up would constitute criminal culpability even if the virus came from the wet market. If the virus came from a lab, Chinese involvement in the cover-up constitutes a crime against humanity.

CHAPTER TWO

ONE HUNDRED DAYS— CHRONICLE OF A LOCKDOWN

Worldwide, the Spanish flu carried off 40 million people, or two percent of humanity, equivalent to more than 150 million people today. . . . So why did this ferocious pandemic fail to wreck the economy? The answer is deceptively simple: for the most part, whether by necessity or choice, people barreled through.

—Walter Scheidel, *Foreign Affairs* (May 28, 2020)

If the epidemic spreads, morals too will broaden, and we may see again the saturnalia of Milan, men and women dancing round the graves.

—Albert Camus, *The Plague* (1948)

THE PAUSE THAT SOLD THE WORLD

Once the virus spread widely in the United States, an economic lockdown was imposed. Was a lockdown necessary given the behavior of the virus? The short answer is no, it wasn't.

The lockdown of the U.S. economy and the end of social intercourse beginning in stages in March 2020 will be viewed as one of the great blunders in history. The lockdown was unnecessary, ineffective, and based on both official deception and bad science. The costs were not considered. Better alternatives were ignored. It was mostly unconstitutional. The American people were treated like not-very-bright children. The lockdown represented rule by experts operating outside their areas of expertise who were revealed to be not that expert even within their fields. Above all, it represented a failure of leadership, as politicians hid behind bureaucrats instead of widening the circle of cognitive diversity and leading from the front.

Before considering these conclusions, the term "lockdown" should be defined. There never was a uniform national lockdown. President Trump had broad emergency powers under numerous statutes, many enacted in the 1950s to help govern America in the event of a nuclear war, yet he used few of them.

Trump banned travel to the United States from China, most of Europe, the UK, Ireland, Brazil, Iran, and other ports of embarkation in a series of proclamations issued between January 31, 2020, and May 24, 2020. President Trump also urged Americans on March 16, 2020, to limit their travel. Trump used the bully pulpit in almost daily press conferences and briefings in March and April 2020 to recommend common-sense actions like social distancing, hand washing, no handshakes, and self-quarantine as needed. Still, none of these recommendations were orders. There was no national lockdown.

Instead the country locked down state by state in fits and starts based on orders from governors, mayors, and other public officials. New York City schools closed on March 15. California started its lockdown on March 19. New York State started its complete lockdown on March 22. Many states locked down in late March. Georgia was among the last states to lock down; it did so on April 3. South Dakota never did.

No two lockdowns were alike. Some orders were draconian, closing all nonessential businesses, ordering individuals to stay at home, requiring face masks for those who had to be outside, closing parks and beaches, banning gatherings of more than a few individuals, and shutting down large parts of public transportation systems. Other states had some but not all of those features, down to South Dakota, which was 100 percent voluntary.

Definitions of "essential" business varied widely. Gun shops were deemed essential in New Hampshire and nonessential in New Jersey. California's lockdown order was ambiguous on gun shops. Still, mayors took it upon themselves to close gun stores. New Jersey and California later both backed down in the face of lawsuits and citizen outrage. Nationwide gun sales skyrocketed in April and the months following.

Some state lockdown orders were simply bizarre. Michigan governor Gretchen Whitmer banned large-store sales of carpets and paint. No one knows why.

Some orders were fatal. On March 25, 2020, New York governor Andrew Cuomo issued an order to nursing home (NH) administrators that stated, "NHs must comply with the expedited receipt of residents returning from hospitals to NHs. . . . No resident shall be denied re-admission or admission to the NH solely based on a confirmed or suspected diagnosis of COVID-19." On April 7, 2020, Governor Cuomo issued a similar order with regard to adult care facilities (ACFs) that read, "No resident shall be denied re-admission or admission to the ACF solely based on a confirmed or suspected diagnosis of COVID-19." Those in nursing homes or adult care facilities are among the most vulnerable to COVID-19 and the most likely to die if infected. The virus spreads most easily in high-density facilities like nursing homes and adult care facilities, accommodations that are incubators for death and disease. The alternative to Cuomo's order would have been a temporary facility set up to quarantine those patients with COVID-19 without sending them back to the nursing homes or adult care facilities where they would infect others. Over 4,500 COVID-19 patients in New York were returned to nursing homes and adult care facilities pursuant to Cuomo's orders. Over 5,800 residents of those homes and facilities in New York died during the outbreak, more than in any other state. Daniel Arbeeny, whose father was a COVID-19 victim who died after being pulled out of a Brooklyn nursing home, said that Cuomo's order "was the single dumbest decision anyone could make if they wanted to kill people."

As inconsistent as the lockdown was, the reopening was no less disjointed. Most states announced relief from the lockdowns as of May 31, 2020. Other states selected reopening dates in June. Some states did not announce reopening dates. Those states with reopening plans often used a Phase 1, Phase 2, Phase 3 approach in which retail businesses might open first, followed by restaurants and bars, and finally beaches and parks. Or not. The defined phases were entirely muddled.

This patchwork approach to closing and then reopening the economy as a form of disease control points to the first objection—it's unnecessary and ineffective. Lockdowns don't work.

If someone in Michigan needs paint and can't get it at a local Home Depot (an essential business), they can simply drive to Ohio and buy all the paint they want. If someone in New Jersey wants to buy a gun and the gun shops are closed, they can simply drive to Pennsylvania. This is not a comment on paint or guns. It's a comment on stopping the spread of disease. Lockdowns don't work.

If an infectious virus is spotted early enough and infections are few and in a confined area, then an extreme quarantine can be effective. During the Spanish flu of 1918, one small military base on an island imposed a total quarantine backed up with armed sentries. It worked; there was no flu on that base. Still, America is not an island, it is not small, and we do not have armed sentries on every street. John M. Barry, author of *The Great Influenza*, a book about the Spanish flu, describes the problem:

> No medicine and none of the vaccines developed then could prevent influenza. The masks worn by millions were useless as designed and could not prevent influenza. Only preventing exposure to the virus could. . . .
>
> Places that isolated themselves—such as Gunnison, Colorado, and a few military installations on islands—escaped. But the closing orders that most cities issued could not prevent exposure; they were not extreme enough. Closing saloons and theaters and churches meant nothing if significant numbers of people continued to climb onto streetcars, continued to go to work, continued to go to the grocer. . . . The virus was too efficient, too explosive, too good at what it did. In the end the virus did its will around the world.

There were ample alternatives to a total lockdown of the economy and social life that could have been implemented. There's nothing wrong with voluntary social distancing, hand washing, and proper masks (most masks don't work for their intended purpose or are worn incorrectly; some can work to prevent viral spread by those already infected who exhibit coughing and sneezing). Voluntary self-quarantine by those most vulnerable or most exposed is a good idea. School closures accomplished little because children have good resistance to SARS-CoV-2. Children don't get COVID-19 from other children, they get it from adults, and they'll encounter more adults at home than in school.

This brings us to the real reason for the lockdown, and the motivation for official fearmongering. The lockdown was never intended primarily to halt the spread of the virus. That's impossible short of martial law and involuntary house arrest of the entire population. In fact, the spread of the virus is desirable in some ways because the fatality rate is quite low and herd immunity (large numbers of survivors with antibodies and immunity) is the best way to stop the pandemic, at least for now. The reason for the lockdown was primarily to "flatten the curve," in the words of Dr. Anthony Fauci, director of the National Institute of Allergy and Infectious Diseases.

What does that mean? Everyday Americans are brighter than elites give them credit. Still, it is too much to expect the typical viewer of a Fauci press conference to be expert in integral calculus. Americans were shown two curves. One curve had a high peak indicating a large number of infections from SARS-CoV-2. The other curve, which was "flattened," had a far small number of infections at the peak. Americans naturally favored the smaller number over the larger number and were persuaded that a near-complete lockdown was needed to flatten the curve and reduce the caseload.

What was not clearly explained (except in scientific journals) was that total infections and deaths would be about the same over time with or without the lockdown. Until a vaccine is created the virus will spread. Flattening the curve means elongating the curve. The peak load is lower, but the duration is longer. Total cases and fatalities are defined by the total area *under* the curve, not by the *height* of the curve at a particular point. A lockdown that flattens the curve does reduce peak patient load on the health-care system, yet it will not reduce total infections and fatalities in the long run. In fact, the lockdown may increase fatalities by delaying herd immunity, which is the only source of immunization and reduced exposure in the absence of a vaccine.

This real rationale of reducing the peak load is revealed in the medical literature. Dr. Michael Mina, associate medical director of clinical microbiology at Boston's Brigham and Women's Hospital, said, "I think the whole notion of flattening the curve is to slow things down so that this doesn't hit us like a brick wall. It's really all borne out of the risk of our health care infrastructure pulling apart at the seams if the virus spreads too quickly and too many people start showing up at the emergency room at any given time."

Reducing the peak load on an overburdened health-care system is a legitimate policy goal. Some victims will die if they cannot receive prompt medical care. Still, there were solutions to this problem other than destroying the U.S. economy. Lockdowns could have been limited by location and time to those areas most likely to be overwhelmed. Care facilities could have been surged in the form of hospital ships and temporary hospitals (as was done in New York City and Los Angeles). Doctors and nurses could have been shifted from low-risk areas to areas of greater need (a common practice during the 1918 Spanish flu). An extreme nationwide lockdown was not needed and did not help.

Even if the case for a broader lockdown was stronger because of the peak load problem, why was this not explained clearly to the American people? Experts and politicians hid behind their flattening charts without making it clear that they were aiming for timing differences, not a long-term reduction in cases or fatalities. Fear was their most effective weapon. Trust was the first victim.

Politicians and public health officials faced the same dilemmas in the Spanish flu epidemic. Author John Barry explains the problem well:

> There was terror afoot in 1918, real terror.
>
> But, as horrific as the disease itself was, public officials and the media helped create that terror—not by exaggerating the disease but by minimizing it, by trying to reassure. . . . For if there is a single dominant lesson from 1918, it's that governments need to tell the truth in a crisis. Risk communication implies

managing the truth. You don't manage the truth. You tell the truth. . . .

The public could trust nothing and so they knew nothing. . . . The fear, not the disease, threatened to break the society apart. As Victor Vaughan—a careful man, a measured man, a man who did not overstate to make a point—warned, civilization could have disappeared within a few more weeks.

So, the final lesson of 1918, a simple one yet one most difficult to execute, is that those who occupy positions of authority must lessen the panic that can alienate all within a society. Society cannot function if it is every man for himself. By definition, civilization cannot survive that.

Another rationale for the lockdown was that it would buy time to create a vaccine. The costs of shutting down the economy would be offset by the lives saved once a vaccine was ready for mass inoculations. This would render the virus almost harmless, end the pandemic, and allow for a relatively risk-free reopening of all facets of the economy.

There's only one problem with this vaccine rationale. An effective vaccine is highly unlikely to appear. Dr. Jay Bhattacharya, professor of medicine at Stanford University, stated the matter succinctly: "There aren't any vaccines for human coronaviruses. . . . We don't have a single vaccine for any of them." Dr. Bhattacharya makes a point that is often lost in the Wall Street chatter and hype about "silver bullets" and "miracle drugs." SARS-CoV-2 is not a flu virus. COVID-19 is not influenza. We are dealing with a new virus and a mysterious disease we do not understand.

It is true that many fatalities from COVID-19 are due to influenza or pneumonia. A new vaccine for either disease would help reduce fatalities from COVID-19. Any one of a number of new drugs under development that reduce discomfiture, improve breathing, or treat severe symptoms are valuable and will make the disease more manageable. Hopefully, those drugs will work as expected. Yet they are not cures. HIV-AIDS is an apt comparison. There are drugs that, when taken in combination, reduce the side effects of AIDS, mitigate symptoms, and allow sufferers to live long and relatively normal lives, provided the drug regimens are followed. That's a blessing. Yet there is no cure for AIDS.

The research efforts aimed at developing a cure for COVID-19 are numerous and well funded. While enormous profits might be made, the motivation now seems to be a genuine desire to save lives and eliminate the pandemic. A cure may be available in early 2021, although some virologists warn it could take far longer. This prospect must be weighed against science's inability yet to devise a cure for any coronavirus. Even a successful vaccine must be judged in the context of viral mutation. Medicine could create a vaccine that produces antibodies for one version of the virus, only to discover the virus mutated into a more lethal form that is unaffected by those antibodies.

Two recent studies, one conducted in China, the other in Spain, indicate that antibodies produced in those infected with SARS-CoV-2 may decrease significantly in as little as three weeks. A contributor to the Spanish study, Raquel Yotti, said, "Immunity can be incomplete, it can be transitory, it can last for just a short time." The implication of these studies is that even if a vaccine is developed, it may be of limited effectiveness if any antibodies produced disappear within weeks. The research should be continued and supported by all means. Yet buying time for research was never a good reason to destroy the economy.

Perhaps the greatest fault of the experts who pushed the lockdown is their utter failure to consider the costs. It would be one thing if the lockdown were free or involved relatively minor inconvenience. In that case, even small gains relative to expectations might have been worth the cost. But lockdowns are not free.

The destruction of over $4 trillion in asset value and the loss of $2 trillion in economic output was the cost of the lockdown. Perhaps epidemiologists and virologists are so embedded in the world of science that they have no familiarity with the real world of economics. If so, it was the obligation of political leaders to take charge and balance competing considerations. The doctors mostly exceeded their authority and the politicians failed to stop them.

Economics aside, there are a host of other costs that argue against a lockdown. The first is immunity loss. While we were all working from home (if we could) to avoid SARS-CoV-2, we were also evading a long list of other viruses and bacteria that we routinely encounter. Those encounters help us to maintain immunities. By staying in place, our immune systems have now weakened. As we venture out again, those viruses and bacteria will be waiting for us. Many will sicken and die because we have squandered our immunities.

The lockdown was implemented to save lives from COVID-19. That's possible in the short run and doubtful in the long run. Yet how many died to save lives? Total deaths from COVID-19 in the United States as of this writing are over 200,000. That number is expected to reach 500,000 in the coming year. Most of those deaths would have occurred with or without the lockdown. Lives saved by the lockdown itself are relatively few, according to the Centers for Disease Control and Prevention (CDC). The latest CDC estimates show a 0.65 percent fatality rate among those who are symptomatic, while estimating a 40 percent rate of asymptomatic cases among the infected. That puts the overall infection fatality rate at 0.39 percent: materially higher than seasonal flu yet lower than the pandemics of 1957, 1968, and 2009, which did not result in lockdowns. Another study published by *The Lancet* reported that "full lockdowns and wide-spread COVID-19 testing were not associated with reductions in the number of critical cases or overall mortality." When it comes to mortality, lockdowns don't work.

What about the social costs of the lockdown?

Findings presented by the American Institute for Economic Research show that there is a 3.6 percent increase in deaths from opioid use for every 1 percent increase in the U.S. unemployment rate (including those out of the labor force). Using a conservative estimate of a 20 percent unemployment rate (including those out of the labor force) in the United States as a result of the lockdown suggests an additional 28,797 deaths from opioid use. Estimates for additional deaths from other drug use, alcohol use, suicide, and domestic violence all attributable to the deleterious effects of the lockdown suggest that perhaps 50,000 or more deaths will result from all causes (drugs, alcohol, suicide, domestic violence) as a direct consequence of the lockdown. Doctors in California have anecdotally confirmed these estimates. Dr. Michael deBoisblanc of the John Muir Medical Center in Walnut Creek, California, said, "The numbers are unprecedented." He has seen a "year's worth of suicides" in just the four weeks ending May 21, 2020.

Lockdown costs don't stop with the trillions of dollars of lost wealth and tens of thousands of lockdown-related deaths. Many have died from heart attacks and cancer by deferring needed medical procedures for fear of contracting COVID-19 in hospitals. There are deleterious mental and physical health outcomes from loneliness, isolation, and despair. Educational progress, especially among the young, was set back. Communities were being destroyed. Entrepreneurs were arrested for cutting hair or opening gyms. Constitutional rights to the free exercise of religion and to life and liberty were denied without due process of law. Petty bureaucrats assumed dictatorial power over people's lives at the federal, state, and local levels. And for what? This destruction of wealth, deprivation of rights, and degradation of communities have been supported by epidemiologists and virologists who know little of law, economics, or sociology and who were empowered by panicked politicians afraid to lead.

Even as straightforward a topic as face masks got caught in the crossfire of expert disagreements. Dr. Anthony Fauci told a reporter on June 16, 2020, "Masks are not 100 percent protective. However, they certainly are better than not wearing a mask." On June 25, 2020, Dr. Tom Frieden, former director of the Centers for Disease Control and Prevention, told the *New York Times*, "You don't need a mask if you're outdoors not near anybody. You don't need a mask if you're in a community that doesn't have Covid." Actually, both experts were correct, with qualifications. Yet no one could blame the public for being confused and mistrustful when they heard apparent contradictions from supposed "experts."

Lockdown supporters have attempted to rebut critics by claiming the critics are, in effect, trading dollars for lives. One of the most outspoken voices for this view is Nobel Prize–winning economist Paul Krugman. In a column entitled "How Many Will Die for the Dow?" he wrote, "Trump and his party want to go full speed ahead with reopening no matter how many people it kills. . . . Their de facto position is that Americans must die for the Dow." As an economist, Krugman did some brilliant work in the 1990s. As a columnist, he has been wrong about almost everything since.

Policy makers calculate trade-offs between potential death and safety and efficiency every day. Lowering the speed limit to forty miles per hour would save lives, but we don't do that because it's costly and inefficient. If you're really concerned about it, you don't have to drive. Plant-safety rules are designed to protect workers, yet extremes are avoided because the work must go on. Workers receive training and are informed of the risks. If you find the risks unacceptable, you're free to work elsewhere. The point is that these trade-offs are made continually both from a policy perspective and through individual choices. Krugman's top-down, doctrinaire approach is typical of academia and shines a light on bureaucracy's tendency toward totalitarian solutions. Reopening the economy will cost some lives and save others. Individuals may choose to remain home, and some should. That's what liberty means.

Finally, what was the scientific basis for the lockdown in the first place? What was the origin of the lockdown plan that carried huge costs and produced so little apparent benefit?

The CDC previewed a plan for what became the lockdown in a paper published November 2006. The paper was coauthored by Robert J. Glass, a complexity analyst at Sandia National Laboratories with no expertise in immunology or epidemiology. Another coauthor was a fourteen-year-old public high school student who had built a complex system model as a class project. The authors acknowledge contributions from Neil Ferguson, a disease modeler at Imperial College London, who resigned from a UK government post after admitting an "error of judgement" and whose pandemic social distancing models have been widely discredited. The CDC paper then became the basis for a 109-page lockdown blueprint published by CDC in February 2007. The 2006 CDC paper and the original 2007 CDC blueprint were in response to requests from President George W. Bush for a plan of action after the avian flu outbreak in 2006. Bush had read a detailed history of the 1918 Spanish flu pandemic during that avian flu outbreak and wanted the government to be prepared in case another pandemic arose. The Bush plan was updated by CDC in 2017 after a five-year review initiated by the Obama administration. Finally, the Trump administration used this plan to implement the lockdown during the 2020 COVID-19 pandemic. What the CDC offered the country was a return to the Middle Ages.

The original sin in this entire policy sequence is that Robert Glass, coauthor of the 2006 paper, was not expert in disease. He was familiar with complexity theory models involving what are called "autonomous agents" (created by computer code) interacting based on preprogrammed response functions to programmed changes in conditions. I've done this type of work at the Los Alamos National Laboratory, not far from Glass's home base at Sandia. It's valuable for simulations and certain types of forecasting but has serious limitations, including the fact that it's done in a black box not involving real humans, and it's weak in its consideration of alternative scenarios and exogenous opportunity costs. The output of Glass's model was worthless because the assumptions in the model were inflexible and ignored human behavior. Humans are geared to resist government dictates and continue social interaction in whatever channels are available. Glass ignored these limitations and developed lockdown models with a rigid, unrealistic set of assumptions. The CDC did the rest.

The paper, blueprint, and update include headings such as "Behavioral Rules" and "Community Mitigation Interventions." The 2017 final plan's checklists include recommendations for "Temporarily closing schools," "Modifying, postponing, or canceling large public events," and "Creating physical distance between people." The entire lockdown scenario was based on specifications worked out through the Bush, Obama, and Trump administrations based on a paper produced by a scientist who knew nothing about disease, behavioral psychology, or economics. This was bureaucracy run amok. And it became our reality, costing lives and destroying trillions of dollars of wealth.

Experts said so at the time. The most powerful voice against the bureaucratic lockdown plan was Dr. D. A. Henderson, a distinguished scholar, Dean of the Johns Hopkins Bloomberg School of Public Health, and recipient of the Presidential Medal of Freedom, awarded in part for his leadership in the successful effort to eradicate smallpox. Henderson coauthored a paper in 2006 that refutes the Glass work and the CDC guidelines. The Henderson paper states, "Historically, it has been all but impossible to prevent influenza from being imported into a country or political jurisdiction, and there has been little evidence that any particular disease mitigation measure has significantly slowed the spread of flu. . . . The negative consequences of large-scale quarantine are so extreme (forced confinement of sick people with the well; complete restriction of movement of large populations . . .) that this mitigation measure should be eliminated from serious consideration. . . . Travel restrictions, such as closing airports . . . have historically been ineffective . . . and will likely be even less effective in the modern era."

At the same time that nonepidemiologists and bureaucrats were going full speed down the lockdown route, serious virologists and epidemiologists were warning that lockdowns don't work. They were right. Henderson and his coauthors supported commonsense measures such as self-quarantine, hand washing, protective gear, and respiratory hygiene. They warned that extreme measures such as a national lockdown don't work. Their conclusions were ignored by the CDC and President Trump's Coronavirus Task Force. The American people paid the price.

The best explanation of the dynamics of a lockdown comes from author Laura Spinney in her history of the Spanish flu, *Pale Rider*. Spinney's point is not that lockdowns *can't* work; it's that they *don't* work because of coercion and mistrust. She writes:

> In a future flu pandemic, health authorities will introduce containment measures such as quarantine, school closures and prohibitions on mass gatherings. These will be for our collective benefit, so how do we ensure that everyone complies? . . . Experience has shown that people have a low tolerance for mandatory health measures, and that such measures are most effective when they are voluntary, when they respect and depend on individual choice, and when they avoid the use of police powers. . . . Using

2016 numbers, . . . more than 3 million Americans would have to die before CDC would advise such a step—a measure of how counterproductive that organisation believes compulsion to be.

But if disease containment works best when people choose freely to comply, then people must be informed about the nature of the disease and the risk it poses. . . .

Censorship and playing down the danger don't work; relaying accurate information in an objective and timely fashion does. . . . Trust is not something that can be built up quickly. If it is not in place when a pandemic declares itself, then however good the information being circulated, it probably won't be heeded.

Spinney wrote this in 2017, before COVID-19. She based it on the lessons of 1918. She recommended voluntarism, individual choice, and avoidance of police powers. She emphasized straight talk and trust. In 2020 leaders used mandatory, not voluntary rules. Police engaged in heavy-handed arrests and roadblocks. Official information gave false reassurance and ignored the dangers. Trust was thin at the beginning of the pandemic and nonexistent at the end. Official actions ignored the lessons of history and the counsel of common sense. The lockdown failure should have come as no surprise.

In the end, did the lockdown save lives? Yes. It probably cost more lives than it saved, yet it did save lives. Martial law would have saved more lives, at least in the short run. And it would have destroyed the country.

Counting lives is not the only test. Lives could have been saved with far less intrusive measures. The government's lockdown plan left no room for voluntary action and common sense. It took no account of exogenous costs, including deaths of despair, reduced immunities, and trillions of dollars in lost wealth and lost output that could have been put to life-saving ends. Dramatic evidence that lockdowns don't work emerged on October 2, 2020, when the White House announced that both President Trump and First Lady Melania Trump tested positive for the virus. The virus goes its way with or without a lockdown. The lockdown was unnecessary and ineffective. It was the ultimate failure of elite expertise. Alternatives were available. The lockdown was a world-historic blunder.

We turn now specifically to the economy, which has borne the brunt of this blunder.

CHAPTER THREE

THE NEW GREAT DEPRESSION

Only a few months into this tragic COVID-19 shock, there are already concerns that Wall Street is once again flourishing while Main Street is suffering. . . . If current asset prices fail to be validated by a decisive economic recovery, the longer-term well-being not just of the economy and markets but of institutions and society as well will be at risk.

—Mohamed A. El-Erian, *Foreign Policy* (May 29, 2020)

M arket crashes typically have an indelible date that imprints the event for future generations. Black Friday, September 24, 1869, is the date an attempted gold-market corner by Jay Gould and Big Jim Fisk collapsed. Black Monday, October 28, 1929, was the date the Dow Jones Industrial Average fell 12.82 percent in one day, triggering what became the first Great Depression. The Dow fell another 11.73 percent the next day, for a two-day 23 percent decline. Another Black Monday occurred on October 19, 1987, when the Dow fell 22.6 percent in one day, the largest single-day percentage decline in history. Most alive today recall September 15, 2008, the day Lehman Brothers collapsed, the largest bankruptcy in U.S. history. Stock market reaction that day was muted; the Dow fell 4.5 percent. That was only the beginning of cascading stock declines that took the Dow down an additional 39 percent before it bottomed on March 6, 2009. While these dates are iconic, they did not occur in isolation. The 1869 gold-corner collapse was preceded by a spike in gold prices as the corner progressed. The October 28, 1929, Black Monday crash was preceded by Black Thursday, October 24, when markets lost 11 percent at the opening bell but recovered to close down about 2 percent for the day. Likewise the stock market was declining long before the Lehman Brothers debacle as news from the sequential collapses of Bear Stearns, Fannie Mae, and Freddie Mac was digested by markets between March and July 2008. Each great crash was preceded by warnings that were mostly ignored.

The New Great Depression dates from February 24, 2020. That's the day the market broke sharply lower, and it did not look back until hitting bottom on March 23, 2020. That completed a precipitous 36 percent decline in the Dow Jones Industrial Average. February 24 was not the all-time high; that happened a few days earlier. And the decline to the March 23 low was not a straight line; there were some up days along the way.

What separated the new Black Monday of February 24 from normal day-to-day market volatility was a shock based on news of the global pandemic. The shock did not come from China; that was old news. The shock came from Italy. Reported cases in Italy went from near zero to seventeen new cases on February 21, forty-two on February 22, and ninety-three on February 23.

On Sunday night, February 23, I tweeted a storm warning:

> Wall St. faces a day of reckoning with coronavirus. No one believes China data. Yet, the market has been encouraged by positive trends in the same data. Which is it?

Meanwhile, firm data from Korea, Japan, Iran & Italy shows
the virus is out of control.

By the time markets opened on February 24, traders had seen the
Italian caseload triple in one day and more than double the next. It was
not the absolute number of cases that spooked traders; they were relatively few. It was exponential growth. That was a sure sign of a pandemic
already out of control that would grow worse. More worrying was the
fact that the disease had clearly jumped from China to Italy. That meant
it could go anywhere in the world and probably already had. It is one
thing to believe that China has a problem that might, hopefully, be contained. It's another to realize the viral spread is uncontained and threatens the entire world. That's what changed before the market opened on
February 24. That's the day the New Great Depression began.

The New Great Depression is a story of numbers in terms of lost
wealth and lost output. More important, it's a story of people in terms of
lost jobs, lost businesses, and broken dreams. Finally, it's a story of the
future in terms of where the economy goes from here. These three facets
are considered below.

THE CRASH

The stock market fell 3.6 percent on Monday, February 24. That was a
small decline compared with the dark days to come and does not even
rank among the twenty largest percentage declines in the Dow's history.
Yet it was ominous in other ways. It signaled a break in the psychology
of market participants. Prior to February 24, down days and up days were
taking turns and market indices were near if not quite at all-time highs.
Markets had learned to live with the "Wuhan flu" and tended to see it as
a China problem that was coming under control. February 24 was the

day market participants opened their eyes, saw the global pandemic for what it was, and started to reprice stocks based on new, more realistic assumptions. Stock markets have a reputation for looking into the future and discounting today's prices based on what they see. There's truth in that, yet it's not the same as saying markets always see clearly. Markets often discount based upon a version of events far removed from reality. When that happens, stress builds between reality and the market's vision. Reality always wins, yet that can take time. A positive narrative about China and COVID-19 prevailed in the markets from late January to February 21. It appeared the caseload was leveling off and the virus might be contained. Over the weekend of February 22–23, Italian data was a reality check on the Chinese chimera. On Monday, February 24, the spell was broken and markets came to grips with the reality of a global viral crisis.

From there the fall was unrelenting. On March 9, 2020, the stock market fell 7.79 percent (2,013 points on the Dow). On March 12, 2020, the stock market fell 9.99 percent (2,352 points on the Dow). On March 16, 2020, the stock market fell 12.93 percent (2,997 points on the Dow). All three moves were among the twenty largest one-day percentage declines in stock market history. The March 12 and March 16 moves were among the five largest one-day declines. The March 16 move was the second-largest one-day decline, larger than both days that started the first Great Depression and larger than any day but the 22.6 percent free fall on October 19, 1987. Trading halts, so-called circuit breakers, implemented in response to the 1987 crash, were triggered repeatedly. If one measures by daily point losses instead of percentage changes, eight of the ten largest one-day point drops in history occurred in February or March 2020. The entire path from the Dow's all-time high of 29,550 on February 12 to the interim low of 18,591 on March 23 was a 37 percent collapse. This was a historic crash. The longest bull market in history was dead.

Wall Street cheerleaders appearing on financial media were quick to point out that this 37 percent crash paled in comparison with the 89.2 percent crash in the Dow during the Great Depression. This statistic conveniently ignores the fact that the 89.2 percent crash took three years (1929–32). The Dow fell 17.2 percent in 1929, 33.8 percent in 1930, 52.7 percent in 1931, and 22.6 percent in 1932. The 37 percent COVID-19 crash didn't take three years; it took less than six weeks. And there was no assurance that there was not worse yet to come.

Stocks staged an impressive rally from late March to early September, regaining almost all of the lost ground. This was trumpeted by the Wall Street crowd as a sign that the worst was over, the economy was reopening quickly, and a solid V-shaped recovery (down fast, up fast) was in the making. History tells a different tale.

On the way to an 89.2 percent decline between 1929 and 1932, the Dow staged some impressive rallies that offered hope to Wall Street that the worst was over. Stocks rose 28.6 percent from November 17, 1929, to April 20, 1930. They rose 13.2 percent from June 22 to September 7, 1930. Stocks rallied again by 17.5 percent from January 18 to February 22, 1931. Finally, stocks rallied 22.2 percent between May 31 and June 28, 1931. These double-digit rallies occurred in the midst of the greatest decline in history. The tape tells the story. The 1929 rally started at Dow 228. The 1930 rally started at Dow 215. The January 1931 rally started at Dow 163. The May 1931 rally started at Dow 128. These rallies (and smaller ones) took place during a slow, relentless fall in the Dow from 380 to 42 by the time of the bottom in July 1932. It's not that rallies don't happen. It's not that some investors don't make money. It is the case that rallies tell you nothing about the long-term trend, which is driven by larger forces than momentum and wishful thinking.

So-called bear-market rallies during the first Great Depression can be explained by both technical factors (in some stages, markets fell so far so fast that a rally seemed appropriate to traders) and fundamental factors (there was occasional good news, based on Herbert Hoover's recovery programs, that justified a pickup in stock prices) even as the backdrop remained dreadful. The same cannot be said about twenty-first-century market rallies in the midst of a mortgage market collapse (2007–8), a record weak recovery (2009–19), and a pandemic (2020). Inflated asset values, especially in stocks, were more the result of passive investing, indexation, exchange-traded funds (a mini-index), stock buybacks (a thinly disguised liquidation of corporate America driven by CEO option packages and technical tax advantages), robots algorithmically programmed to "buy the dips," and, above all, Federal Reserve money printing and a broadly applied too-big-to-fail mentality that simply would not allow markets to fall. In this environment, investors could scarcely be blamed for going along for the ride.

These twenty-first-century contrivances are not sustainable. Passive investing and indexing run out of steam when there are no more active investors to engage in price discovery. Stock buybacks dry up when leverage is not available and corporate cash flows erode. Robots will be the only buyers ahead of a fall when real money moves to the sidelines. The coding crowd can move on to other pursuits. The Fed will find that money printing is not stimulus when velocity is crashing for psychological reasons that the Fed scarcely comprehends. The game is up. All that is left are the larger forces of pandemic, unemployment, and fear for the future.

The index pattern for the S&P 500 reflects these facts. The index hit an all-time high of 3,386 on February 19, 2020. Then it began to crash in response to the spreading COVID-19 pandemic. It took a second plunge (after a slight rebound) on March 4 in response to a spiking caseload and soaring unemployment. The index bottomed on March 23 at 2,237, down 33 percent from the high, then began an impressive rally to 3,580 by September 2, a 60 percent surge off the lows and a new all-time high.

The S&P is a cap-weighted index, which means that stock prices of companies with a larger market capitalization have a disproportionate impact on the performance of the overall index. The market cap heavyweights in the S&P 500 are the familiar tech giants—Amazon, Apple, Microsoft, Netflix, Facebook, and Alphabet (better known as Google). What those stocks have in common is limited reliance on physical retail space. Apple has stores, yet they are as much showrooms and consulting boutiques as sales outlets. Amazon owns Whole Foods, yet that is a play on home delivery ordered through the Amazon portal. Otherwise, these companies are largely online digital firms offering software, streaming services, search, advertising, and the like. Given the cap-weighted dominance of these firms, it would be more realistic to call the S&P 500 the S&P 6.

A similar pattern emerges from the list of thirty companies in the Dow Jones Industrial Average index. This list is not cap weighted but is calculated according to a complicated proprietary formula. Still, the list includes tech firms such as Apple, Cisco, IBM, Intel, and Microsoft. It also includes telecommunications and media firms like Verizon and Disney and financial firms like American Express, Goldman Sachs, JPMorgan Chase, Travelers, and Visa. Together those firms make up 40 percent of the Dow names. While no business was untouched by the pandemic, technology, telecommunications, media, and finance were affected far less than firms in manufacturing, transportation, and retail. Similarly, the NASDAQ Composite is a famously tech-heavy index. In short, our major stock indices are divorced from the real economy and relatively unscathed by 60 million newly unemployed Americans and the near wipeout of small and medium-sized enterprises.

Stocks are not traded by humans today; they're overwhelmingly traded by robots. The robots are trained to read headlines, follow orders, and act instantaneously. Fundamentals don't matter (at least in the short run). If the algorithm tells the robot to "buy the index on stimulus," then every time Fed chairman Jay Powell speaks out, the robots buy the index. If the algorithm tells the robot to "buy the index on more deficit spending," then every time Mitch McConnell and Nancy Pelosi shake hands (or bump elbows) on a new spending deal, the robots buy the index. Robots don't think, don't analyze, and don't look ahead. They just follow orders.

Eventually reality intrudes. Bankruptcy is a wake-up call even for robots. Americans may not understand second-wave viral dynamics, but they understand bankruptcy. They may be affected by it directly; if your employer goes bankrupt or your stock goes to zero, you understand it all too well. Even unaffected Americans sense their company may be next in the queue. Perhaps they'll lose a job next month, or their stock portfolio will deflate as individual holdings go under.

Depressions are more than statistics. A depression is the incalculable sum of individual traumas from job losses and concerns about paying the rent, putting food on the table, securing health care, and helping children get a good education. Job losses do not affect only paychecks; they affect dignity, self-confidence, and prospects for the future. And depressions are more than job losses. Businesses are destroyed or at best disrupted. Ripples extend from there to communities and entire cities. The impact of a depression is deep and long lasting; it may be intergenerational, as was the case with the first Great Depression.

Still, statistics can help us gauge the depth of the depression as a way to understand how people, businesses, and communities have been affected and how badly. They also make the point that this is a depression and not another recession. The 2008 and 1929 financial crises don't offer a meaningful baseline. Market panics of 1998 and 1987, while dangerous to global financial stability, rapidly abated, and relatively few were directly affected. This depression is different, and data helps us to understand why.

The first and most obvious point is that over 60 million Americans lost jobs between March 1 and October 1, 2020. Notions that these job losses will be recovered quickly are false. Job losses will slow at first and then stop. A recovery will begin. That does not mean that 60 million Americans go back to work. Adding over 1 million jobs per month (a huge number by historical standards) for the next three years would barely be enough to take total employment levels back to where they were in February 2020. Even that projection (and it's dubious) misses the point that many lost jobs are *never* coming back. A restaurant that shut its doors during the lockdown and laid off twenty employees will not hire back all twenty the day it reopens. It'll rehire perhaps ten and wait to see how things go. They will likely not go well. Social distancing means fewer tables will be set out and fewer diners allowed inside. The diners themselves will not flock back to restaurants because of residual fear. Of course, this assumes the restaurant does reopen its doors; many won't, they're out of business forever. Meanwhile, the waiters and bartenders not hired back will lose skills and networks, and some will drift from the labor force entirely to the point where, while not technically unemployed as the government defines it, they are unemployed as common sense would see it.

The restaurant case is real, yet it's merely one example. The hashtag #WFH (working from home) became ubiquitous during the lockdown. Millions were WFH. Employers noticed and decided that model works better than crowding employees into ten floors in a midtown office tower, with the logistics that entails, not to mention one million hours of annual commuting time and millions of dollars for rent, insurance, and maintenance. The new office model will be a few floors with shared meeting spaces, offices reserved by the day, and a small staff of receptionists and facilitators. Employees will have lockers for items needed in the offices when they are present; they'll stow their gear in the lockers when they leave. Otherwise, they'll work from home. That's fine for employers. What about the empty office space; landlords' rent; laid-off cleaning staff; lost sales at food trucks, street vendors, and restaurants; half-empty trains and buses; and lunch-hour shopping? That's all gone, or reduced by perhaps 80 percent. Life will go on, yet ancillary jobs and output will not. This is the difference between depressions and recessions. In depressions, things don't get back to normal because there is no normal anymore.

This is not speculation; it's already in the data. In May 2020, only 32 percent of retail stores were paying rent. The rent-payment levels for other industries were: restaurants and bars, 32 percent; hotels and other lodging, 18 percent; gyms and fitness establishments, 26 percent; automotive sales and service businesses, 29 percent; hair and nail salons, 25 percent. The nonpayment data were similarly dismal across other business categories. Dismissing these establishments as small business is blind. Small and medium-sized enterprises host almost 50 percent of all jobs and produce 45 percent of all goods and services in GDP. Collectively they're far more important than Apple, Microsoft, Facebook, and Google combined when it comes to jobs and output. Not paying rent now means these firms are going out of business (at worst) or will be renegotiating leases (at best). This is not healed by deficit spending, money printing, or a rising stock market. These are painful semipermanent losses.

The lockdown lasted one hundred days in most localities yet lingers indefinitely in others. How long can a typical business pay its bills from cash balances with no new revenues received? For restaurants, the limit is sixteen days. For retail stores, it's nineteen days. For professional services such as lawyers and accountants, it's thirty-three days. Personal services businesses such as salons and stylists can last twenty-one days. There are numerous other business categories; the mean figure for all small businesses is twenty-seven days. Small businesses typically do not carry large working capital balances. They rely on revenues to pay staff and vendors and have a small cash cushion. The fact that the lockdown lasted longer than the cash balances could support means that small businesses either closed their doors (conserving available cash despite zero revenue) or borrowed to bridge the gap, or they went broke.

These estimates have played out in real life. On September 21, 2020, the *New York Post* reported that almost 90 percent of New York City bars and restaurants could not pay their August rent. The popular service directory and review website Yelp reported that 97,966 of its business listings were marked "permanently closed" between March 1 and August 31, 2020.

Outside certain localities for brief periods following natural disasters or catastrophes like the 9/11 attacks or the Civil War, this has never happened in U.S. history. There were business failures during the first Great Depression, yet no across-the-board lockdown. There was no widespread business lockdown during the 1918 Spanish flu pandemic (some large gatherings such as sporting events were banned in certain cities). An estimated 50 million to 100 million people died during the Spanish flu, yet the global economy continued and the postpandemic business expansion was strong in most developed economies. What has happened to the U.S. economy because of COVID-19 is unheard of.

While small business bears the lockdown's brunt and revenue losses, large businesses are scarcely immune. Large-business bankruptcies (liabilities of $50 million or more) in May 2020 were higher than in any month of May since 2009. Yet May 2009 came at the end of the 2007–9 recession, when remedies were exhausted and cash had dwindled. May 2020 is near the start of the New Great Depression; large bankruptcy filings will surge in the months ahead. Already this depression has claimed business icons Brooks Brothers, J. C. Penney, Pier 1 Imports, J. Crew, Neiman Marcus, Hertz, Frontier Communications, Chesapeake Energy, and Gold's Gym. Bankruptcy lawyers confirm they are working on more potential filings. Most of these bankruptcies are not liquidations; they fall into the reorganization category. This means the bankrupt company can keep its doors open and operate its business, while creditors are frozen in place by operation of law and cannot pursue claims except under judicial supervision. A bankruptcy plan of reorganization typically includes mass layoffs, plant closures, broken leases, and diminished pensions and benefits. The business may go on but the jobs and supply chains still suffer. Again, these are permanent losses; there is no quick bounce-back from bankruptcy.

Other economic performance measures were no better. On June 8, 2020, the National Bureau of Economic Research (NBER), a private but acknowledged arbiter of recessions, declared that the U.S. economy entered a recession in February 2020. Of course, that refers to a technical recession only; the declaration says nothing about a depression, which is a far more serious matter that completely escapes the notice of the NBER. Pending home sales in the U.S. plunged 35 percent on a year-over-year basis in May 2020. That was a bigger collapse than occurred in the 2007–9 mortgage crisis. Ward's Automotive Survey showed U.S. auto sales crashed from just under seventeen million cars (annualized) in March to fewer than nine million cars (annualized) in April, a 47 percent plunge in one month. Auto sales bounced back to just over twelve million cars in May, but that was still 30 percent below the pre-COVID level. The Institute for Supply Management's Purchasing Managers' Index for manufacturing dropped from an index level of 51.0 in March 2020, barely expansionary, to 43.1 in May, which shows a severe contraction.

The U.S. Commerce Department reported a $49.4 billion U.S. trade deficit for April 2020. A trade deficit is a drag on GDP. Yet that's not the important part of the international trade report. The deficit is simply the net of exports minus imports. Exports fell by 20.5 percent in April compared with March, while imports fell 13.7 percent in the same period. Trade surpluses or deficits don't matter as much as the *level* of world trade. The highly regarded economic research firm Capital Economics reported on June 25, 2020, that April world trade data revealed the "sharpest monthly contraction in world trade on record." We are witnessing the widespread collapse of world trade. Contracting world trade measured by global exports (rather than national surpluses or deficits) was a defining condition of the first Great Depression. It's happening again in the New Great Depression.

U.S. GDP contracted at a 5 percent annualized rate in the first quarter of 2020. That decline was steeper than the 4.4 percent drop in the first quarter of 2009, in the depths of the 2007–9 recession. The fall in the first quarter of 2020 was cushioned by relatively good performance in January and February, which highlights the depths of the March collapse.

Second quarter U.S. GDP reported on July 30, 2020, was a disaster: the worst recorded economic performance in U.S. history. Real GDP fell 32.9 percent on an annualized basis; on a standalone basis (not annualized), GDP fell 9.5 percent, also the worst on record. Applying that rate of decline for a single quarter to a $22 trillion economy yields over *$2.1 trillion in lost output* in the second quarter. That does not compare to 2008–9. That does not compare to 1929–33. This fall was far worse. It's the largest amount of lost output in a single quarter in the history of the United States. It amounts to $6,365 of lost income per person for every man, woman, and child in the United States. It comes to over $25,000 of lost income for every family of four. There has never been anything like it.

Buried in the second quarter GDP report was another sobering statistic: the inflation adjustment was negative 2.1 percent, which means deflation has arrived. Nominal GDP was actually worse than real GDP; the real number got a lift from the deflation. This means debtors, beginning with the United States itself, fared even worse than the economy because deflation increases the real value of debt. Persistent deflation points in the direction of default.

The U.S. crisis must be seen in the broader context. The depression is global; the situation is no better abroad. Projected GDP declines for the full year 2020 in Europe are: Germany, down 6.5 percent; Greece, down 9.7 percent; Spain, down 9.4 percent; France, down 8.2 percent; Italy, down 9.5 percent. For the euro area as a whole, growth for 2020 is projected to fall 7.7 percent. The GDP of the European Union prior to the pandemic was $18.7 trillion. A 7.7 percent projected decline implies $1.44 trillion of lost output in 2020 compared with 2019. That's $3,230 of lost income per person for every man, woman, and child in the European Union, or $12,900 of lost income for a family of four. This is comparable to the destruction at the end of World War II.

The International Monetary Fund concurs with this dismal assessment of global growth. On June 24, 2020, the IMF released its revised forecast for global growth in 2020. The revised outlook called for an 8 percent drop in U.S. GDP for the full year, the worst U.S. decline since the demobilization following the Second World War. The IMF also projected global growth would decline 3.9 percent in 2020. That's the worst global performance since the Great Depression of the 1930s. These forecasts are completely at odds with the "pent-up demand," fast-growth narrative emanating from the White House. The IMF forecasts are likely far more accurate than those coming from the White House and are consistent with analyses from other expert sources.

Lost output means more than lost revenue for business and lost income for individuals. It also means lost sales taxes and income taxes for state and local governments and lost income taxes, excises, and tariffs for the federal government. The impact is already being felt. On June 24, 2020, New York City mayor Bill de Blasio warned that the city might have to lay off 22,000 municipal employees in a matter of months. That would be the first municipal-worker layoff since 2012 and the largest since the city faced bankruptcy in the 1970s.

We'll look closely at the monetary and fiscal response to the New

Great Depression in the next chapter. Still, the simple observation that government revenues are drying up at a time when expenditures for unemployment benefits, health care, emergency responders, police, and other emergency needs are skyrocketing puts governments at all levels into multibillion-dollar deficits (or multitrillion-dollar deficits at the federal level), with no early hope of recovery.

Wall Street pundits point to the stock market as proof that the economy is bouncing back sharply and a strong recovery is right around the corner. The stock market did recover almost all of its pandemic-related losses with a strong performance from late April through early September 2020. Yet this says nothing about an economic recovery. The stock market is divorced from the real economy at this stage. Price discovery that does take place is conducted by robots programmed to "buy the dips," chase headlines, and reinforce any form of momentum. The stock indices are dominated by a handful of companies that have been relatively immune to the hardship that is facing most individuals and firms. The April to September 2020 stock market speaks to the prospects for technology and finance, at least in the short run, yet says nothing about unemployment, growth, collapsing government cash flows, and the way forward.

The New Great Depression is here. The data tells the story. The stock market does not agree; it will eventually. The real story is told by the depression's impact on people's lives. We turn to that topic now.

THE PEOPLE

Americans may or may not be ready for the second wave of SARS-CoV-2, but they are certainly *not* ready for a second wave of layoffs and unemployment. It's coming.

The pandemic-caused depression led to a layoff wave unprecedented in U.S. history. As remarkable as the number of layoffs was the speed with which they occurred. Unemployment in 2020 reached depression levels in three months, compared with three years during the first Great Depression. As bad as that was, some analysts were quickly relieved. At least the worst was over and the U.S. could look forward to recovering those lost jobs and getting to more typical levels of unemployment, if not the extraordinarily low levels of the prepandemic years. Yet the best evidence points to the opposite conclusion.

Unemployment reached 13.3 percent on May 31, 2020, and then fell to 7.9 percent by September 30, 2020. There's no reason to believe the unemployment rate will decline sharply from that level or get anywhere near full employment for years. There are two reasons for this. The first is that the economy was weak before the pandemic. White House claims of "the greatest economy in history" were true only if you counted nominal GDP, in which case that claim is almost always true—and meaningless. What matters, and what Americans care about, is real growth, because that's how jobs are created, businesses grow, and innovation takes place. Annual growth during the last expansion (2009–19) averaged 2.2 percent, the weakest expansion in U.S. history. Most annual growth figures were very close to that average, with no years showing even 3 percent growth. Importantly, there was no material difference between growth in the Trump years of the expansion (2017–19) and in the Obama years (2009–16). This 2.2 percent growth compares with 3.2 percent growth for the average of all expansions since 1980. In the 1950s and 1960s, the average annual growth rate was above 4 percent.

The U.S. economy was weak before the pandemic. Many businesses were barely getting by; many more were contemplating bankruptcy. The pandemic was a perfect opportunity for weak businesses to conduct mass layoffs, file for bankruptcy, close locations, or close their doors completely. The first wave of layoffs (March–June 2020) was hurried. The second wave of layoffs (from October 2020 through 2021) will be more studied.

The first layoff wave was aimed at lower-paid workers, including retail clerks, hospitality workers, restaurant and bar servers, salon workers and stylists, automobile sales associates, baristas, and those in large swaths of the gig economy.

In the second wave, it takes longer to identify the weakest performers and assess the first wave of lost output. That process is now under way; more pink slips are coming. The second wave will target more highly paid professionals, including lawyers, accountants, bankers, nurses, real estate brokers, midlevel managers, state and municipal employees, and developers. Some employees will be terminated due to slack demand for services ancillary to the overall economic collapse. If fewer cars and houses are being purchased, it takes fewer lawyers and bankers to close deals. Others will be laid off because the tax base needed to support them has been badly eroded. States and localities cannot run budget deficits or print money like the federal government. When revenue dries up (as it has), these jobs are jettisoned quickly. Other jobs will be lost because they are upstream from affected businesses. If a restaurant closes its doors, the waiters and cooks are laid off immediately. It takes time for farmers, fishermen, drivers, laundries, and other service providers who support restaurants to feel the effects. That time has passed, and layoffs in those upstream sectors are coming quickly. It's not a static situation; it's highly dynamic. As layoffs spread in the white-collar and upstream segments, those individuals reduce their demand for restaurants and gyms, which feeds back into hard times for the sectors already hard hit. This feedback loop is what distinguishes a depression from a mere recession.

Another headwind for a jobs recovery is the fact that many blue-collar workers laid off in the first wave are slightly better off, at least in the short run, due to government benefits. The Congressional Budget

Office reported on June 4, 2020, that 80 percent of those receiving unemployment benefits will receive more money from unemployment checks than they would expect to receive if they were employed. That is a criticism of neither benefits policy nor individual recipients. It's simply a fact that will impede a rapid jobs recovery. Workers will choose to receive benefits rather than look for work or go back to former jobs even if they become available. This government data is consistent with ample anecdotal evidence from restaurateurs and others planning to reopen their doors who report that their workers don't want to come back to work. It is also consistent with the fact that across-the-board government benefits in the form of onetime checks ($1,200 for adults, $500 for children) and Payroll Protection Plan loans under the 2020 CARES Act were significantly greater than lost personal income in March and April 2020. The checks and CARES Act loans were onetime rescues and will not replace lost income on a sustainable basis as the depression drags on. Yet these payments have cushioned the immediate impact of the mass layoffs, as intended. The problem is that the worst effects of the layoffs and lost income lie ahead, not behind.

One dramatic demonstration of exactly was has happened to jobs in this economy comes from a study of total employment in the United States from 2003 to 2020. Job growth begins with a steady recovery from the 2001 recession. Total employment grew from 130 million jobs in 2003 to 137 million by mid-2007. In the global financial crisis, the United States lost 9 million jobs from mid-2007 to late 2009. By 2010, total employment was back to where it had been in 2003, but no higher. It's as if job growth had stood still for six years. Over the next ten years, the United States gained over 20 million jobs, first under the Obama administration, then during the first three years of the Trump administration. The long recovery (2009–19) was weak, but it was steady—the longest continuous economic expansion recorded in U.S. history.

Then came the New Great Depression. The United States lost over 60 million jobs from March to September 2020. Total employment is now back to levels last seen in the 1990s. It's as if job growth had been on hold for three decades. This setback took only six months.

This level of job losses defies description. While it's easy to recite statistics, it's impossible to convey the human impact. Every job loss is an individual trauma, throwing each laid-off worker into a highly stressful situation: wondering whether they can feed their family, pay the mortgage, and meet obligations for health care or school tuition. When that trauma is expanded by perhaps seventy million (taking into account not just the unemployed worker but also her family members), one begins to get some sense of the magnitude of the collective trauma that has struck America.

An even longer perspective adds to the sense that we are in a new depression. Consider job losses in every recession since 1948, a comparison that includes severe recessions in 1973–75 and 1981–82 and the 2008 global financial crisis. Each of those three recessions was cited as the "worst since the Great Depression" at the time they occurred. That was true at the time; that truth was superseded by the later recessions, which got worse. While those record recessions stand out (along with severe recessions in 1949 and 1958), none bears comparison to the 2020 New Great Depression. Job losses now are greater than those in *the last four recessions combined.*

There's an even more disturbing reality than total job losses. This is the income distribution of the newly unemployed. Less than 10 percent of 2020 job losses have hit those in the top 20 percent income bracket. About 55 percent of total job losses have hit those in the lowest 40 percent income brackets, with about 35 percent of total job losses concentrated in the lowest 20 percent income bracket alone.

Blue-collar jobs are the backbone of the real economy. These workers are the ones on whom we all depend for restaurant meals, hotel accommodations, dry-cleaning services, banking transactions, and the countless everyday interactions that make up our lives. Small and medium-sized enterprises (SMEs) contribute 45 percent of GDP and provide almost 50 percent of total employment. By gutting these jobs, we have gutted the U.S. economy in ways that may take a decade to repair.

Another disturbing trend is the steep decline in labor-force participation. This is slightly more technical than the unemployment rate yet may be more important in terms of the long-term growth potential of the U.S. economy.

When the unemployment rate is announced monthly, whether it's the near-record low 3.4 percent unemployment rate prior to the pandemic or the highest levels of unemployment since the late 1940s announced in May and June 2020, the rate is calculated in a narrowly defined way. The denominator is the total workforce. The numerator is the number of people in the workforce who do not have jobs but are seeking them. Dividing unemployed job seekers by the total workforce (including job seekers) gives us the unemployment rate that receives great attention in financial media.

What if you have no job and you're not actively seeking one? The government doesn't count you. You're not unemployed (even if you have no job) because you're not actively seeking a job. For that matter, you're not even counted as being in the workforce for the same reason. It's as if you didn't exist.

Still, you do exist and you have no job. The person who has no job and does not claim to be seeking one is counted in a different statistical category called the labor-force participation rate (LFPR). The LFPR is calculated in a simpler manner than the unemployment rate. Everyone who could perform a job (whether you're looking for one or not) is in the denominator. Everyone who does have a job is counted in the numerator.

It's basically the number of job holders divided by every adult with or without a job, regardless of intention or motivation to get one.

The steep increase from a 60 percent LFPR in the 1970s to an LFPR over 67 percent in the late 1990s represents the rise of women in the workforce and the rising workforce participation of the baby-boom generation. There will always be those not pursuing traditional jobs for a long list of perfectly good reasons. These non–job holders could be students, homemakers, early retirees, convalescents, or off-the-books handymen paid in cash who do not report the income. An LFPR over 67 percent is considered quite high in a developed economy and a sign of economic strength. That's where the United States was in 2000, at the end of the Clinton boom years.

The LFPR then began a steady decline. This was attributable to both the 2001 recession and the 2008 global financial crisis. Also, demographic factors came into play as the older baby boomers began to retire. Declining health (due to rising obesity, diabetes, drug addiction, etc.) and increased incarceration rates pushed more workers to the sidelines. By 2015, the LFPR had fallen to around 62.4 percent. For the next five years, the LFPR moved in a narrow range between 62.4 percent and 63.5 percent, with a slight upward bias.

Almost overnight, the 2020 New Great Depression slammed the LFPR down to 61.4 percent by September 30, 2020, about where it was in 1970. Again it was as if the U.S. economy had been transported in a time machine to where it was fifty years earlier. A half century of gains for women, minorities, and the disadvantaged were wiped out in the blink of an eye.

This news will get worse. The U.S. Bureau of Labor Statistics (BLS), which computes both the unemployment rate and the LFPR, has admitted it cannot keep up with the sudden flood of applications for unemployment benefits and the household surveys used to calculate the headline rates due to sheer volume, late reports from the states, and classification problems. The BLS has warned analysts to expect major data revisions when it begins to catch up with its backlog. These revisions will mean both higher unemployment rates and lower labor-force participation rates. Both are bad news for U.S. economic growth going forward.

There's a simple way to think about total output. Just take the total number of people working and measure worker productivity on average. That's it. How many people are working and how productive are they? That's all you really need to know.

Productivity doesn't move much in a mature economy. Still, it can change. Lately, productivity has been declining slightly for reasons economists don't entirely understand. It may have to do with an aging demographic or the fact that we use technology to waste time instead of getting work done. Productivity is one reason that economic growth had been slow for the ten years prior to the pandemic.

The main driver of growth since 2000 has been the size of the labor force. *That's what the labor-force participation rate measures.* Once you drop out of the labor force (regardless of the reason), your productivity drops to zero because you're not working. The sharp decline in labor-force participation from 2007 to 2010 coincided with lost output from the global financial crisis and recession. The LFPR rebounded slightly from 2010 to 2019, which was consistent with steady if unspectacular growth.

Now labor-force participation has collapsed. The reported data have not caught up with the reality. LFPR is likely to fall further, to 61 percent or lower. This is partly because some currently unemployed will decide they are retired or can't get jobs and simply drop out of the labor force.

These losses will not be temporary, as unemployment sometimes is. These losses will be permanent as skills, social networks, and references dry up. This is catastrophic. It means that even as businesses reopen and some unemployed get jobs back, others are never coming back to the workforce. Output will be permanently impaired even if productivity picks up a little. The drop in LFPR has been a cliff dive. The economy is underwater as a result; output will remain submerged, perhaps for decades.

Most Americans have a sense of where the economy is. They've heard of shocking spikes in the unemployment rate and in initial claims for unemployment benefits. They know about the lockdown, that businesses everywhere are closed, that the government has asked them to remain home, go out as little as possible, and wear face masks when they do. While this is understood, it is not internalized. It has happened so quickly that Americans are barely over the shock of shutting down the economy. They have not had time to make sense of it or consider the implications. Above all, no one knows what happens next. Will the economy reopen soon? Will life get back to normal by late 2021? Or will the lockdown drag on, at least in some places? Importantly, will a second wave of COVID-19 strike the country and the world later this year? Will that second wave be even more lethal than the peak wave we've just lived through?

A second wave is exactly what happened in the 1918 Spanish flu pandemic. A deadly infectious wave struck from March to June 1918. It went around the world and killed millions. Yet that wave was almost mild compared with the second wave, which struck in October 1918. The second wave was so lethal that dead bodies were piled like cordwood in the streets of major American cities like Philadelphia as government broke down and local authorities could not remove the bodies fast enough. Cities ran out of caskets and space in morgues and resorted to mass graves, with bodies wrapped in sheets and covered only in disinfectant powder.

As for a second wave of COVID-19, almost no official wants to talk about it publicly; few even understand what it means. A second wave of infections is not caused by a return of exactly the same virus. It is caused by a mutation or genetic recombination that can create a new variant even more lethal than the original form of the virus. History and science say we should expect it, yet almost no one is prepared. Most assumed the country would be past the plague by late 2020. There is no certainty in that forecast. A more lethal wave in 2021 is an open possibility.

Independent of a true viral second wave, lockdowns in many cities are being reimposed as quickly as they were lifted. Spain reimposed a lockdown on July 17, 2020, just four weeks after it lifted its initial state of emergency. One bar owner in Barcelona said, "If they impose another lockdown and force us to close, I will drop the blind, but it might as well be dropping the blade of a guillotine on my own neck because we won't be able to survive."

As for a rapid economic bounce-back, the 2020 White House happy-talk brigade, led by economic adviser Larry Kudlow, said all will be well. They spoke of "pent-up demand" that will come roaring back to restore jobs and business profits in a matter of months. They spoke of a soaring economy in 2021. Don't bet on it.

In the first place, many businesses that closed for the lockdown will never reopen. That's not merely because of lockdown orders; it's because they're broke and out of business. On July 23, 2020, the *Washington Post* reported that "as the healthiest businesses have reopened and the ranks of permanent casualties have swelled, it's now more likely than not that a closed business is gone for good." The owners may start a new business someday, somewhere, but the old business is gone. The assets are up for sale at fire-sale prices. The employees will never get their old jobs back. The lease is broken and the storefront vacant. That's the reality for much of America.

The *New York Times* has described the impact of the pandemic on the New York City economy as the equivalent of a "heart attack." The Partnership for New York City, a nonprofit organization of almost three hundred CEOs, reported: "It will be far more difficult to restart and repair the economy than it was to shut it down. The attractions that New Yorkers value most in the city—its cultural, social, and entertainment assets—will remain at least partially shuttered until next year. As many as a third of the 230,000 small businesses that populate neighborhood commercial corridors may never reopen."

These trends are playing out in real time. The number of people who say they are "spending less" has jumped from 32 percent to 51 percent in just a few months. The number of people who say they are "spending more" has plunged from 32 percent to 21 percent. The spread between "spending less" and "spending more" has widened to 30 percentage points, the widest spread since the aftermath of the 2008 crisis.

This trend toward more saving and less spending began in late 2019, even before the pandemic. It's as if Americans saw the recent crash coming. Perhaps some did. It's probably more reflective of the fact that the economy was weak even *before* the pandemic. What that means is that the spread should widen even more. Savings will soar and spending will contract sharply.

That's a smart strategy for individual citizens worried about jobs and their portfolios. Still, it's a disaster for economic recovery, at least in the short run. A high savings rate makes mincemeat out of forecasts from most media prognosticators and public officials. There will be no sharp, fast bounce-back for the economy. Growth will emerge, yet it will be slow. The recovery will be long, hard, and painful for affected individuals, entrepreneurs, and those seeking a job. College graduates in 2020 and 2021 will bear more than their fair share of the burden as entry-level job openings evaporate as employers struggle even to rehire the existing workforce.

THE PROGNOSIS

The depth of the new depression is clear. What is unclear to most observers is the nature and timing of the recovery. The answer is that high unemployment will persist for years, and the United States will not regain 2019 output levels until 2023; growth going forward will be even worse than the weakest-ever growth of the 2009–19 recovery. This may not be the end of the world, yet it is far worse than the most downbeat forecasts. The evidence to support this outlook is in plain sight.

Some sixth-grade math is a good place to begin the analysis. Make 2019 economic output 100 (the actual figure is $22 trillion; "100" is 100 percent of that number; a convenient way to measure ups and downs). Assume output drops 20 percent over the second and third quarters of 2020 (many estimates project larger drops; 20 percent is a plausible if conservative estimate). A 20 percent drop for six months equals a 10 percent drop for the full year, assuming the first and fourth quarters are flat on net. A 10 percent drop from 100 = 90 (or $2.2 trillion of lost output).

Since 1948, U.S. annual real growth in GDP has never exceeded 10 percent. Since 1984, real growth has never exceeded 5 percent. The highest-growth years since the end of World War II were 8.7 percent in 1950, 8 percent in 1951, and 7.2 percent in 1984. An assumption that real growth will occur in 2021 at a 6 percent annual rate is a generous if unrealistic assumption. Such growth would qualify as a V-shaped recovery.

If our new base is 90 (compared with 100 in 2019) and we increase output by 6 percent in 2021, this brings total output to 95.4. If we enter 2022 with the new base of 95.4 and increase that base by 4 percent (so, 95.4 × 1.04), we come to 99.2 in total output by the end of 2022.

Here's the problem. Using 100 as a baseline for 2019 output, and assuming 6 percent real growth in 2021 and 4 percent in 2022 (rates of growth that have not happened on an annual basis since 1984), the economy does not get back to 2019 output levels. The hard truth is that 99.2 < 100. It would take the highest annual real growth in over forty years, sustained for two consecutive years, to get close to 2019 output levels. It would be more realistic to assume real growth will be less than 4 percent per annum. That puts the economy well into 2023 before reaching output levels last achieved in 2019.

A study by the UCLA Anderson School of Management agrees with this estimate. Its study, released on June 24, 2020, estimates that real GDP growth in the United States will be 5.3 percent in 2021 and 4.9 percent in 2022, not enough to achieve even 2019 levels of output. The Anderson forecast says, "We are forecasting a 42% annual rate of decline in real GDP for the current quarter, followed by a . . . recovery that won't return the level of output to the . . . 2019 peak until early 2023." That's the reality of a depression. It's not about continuously declining GDP. A depression is an initial collapse so large that even years of high growth don't dig the economy out of its hole.

Analysts debate the recovery's strength using letters that mimic the shape of a growth curve as shown on a graph. A V-shaped recovery goes down steeply and back up steeply to get output back where it started in a relatively brief time. A U-shaped recovery goes down steeply, does not grow materially right away, and then makes a sharp rise. An L-shaped recovery goes down steeply, followed by low growth for an indefinite period of time. Finally, a W-shaped recovery goes down steeply, bounces back quickly, then falters for a second time before finally recovering and getting back to earlier levels of output and growth.

The 1983–86 recovery from the 1982 recession was a classic V shape. The 1982 recession was severe, yet growth in 1983–86 was extremely strong, and the economy made up the lost output and returned to its prerecession trend line.

A W-shaped recovery is rare, yet the United States arguably experienced just that in the period 1980–83. From 3.2 percent real growth in 1979, the economy suffered a mild recession in 1980, then had a good recovery in 1981, another recession in 1982, and a strong recovery in 1983. That down-up-down-up pattern forms the W.

A U-shaped recovery is a good description of the 1944–48 transition from a wartime economy to a civilian economy. Growth was 8.0 percent in 1944 at the height of the war years. The United States then had a three-year stretch of declining real GDP from 1945 to 1947 as war industries wound down and returning vets flooded the labor market. This recessionary stage was followed by a strong recovery with 4.1 percent growth in 1948. The years 1945, 1946, and 1947 were the elongated, flat bottom of the U.

Finally, the long 2009–19 expansion was an example of an L-shaped recovery. The 2007–9 recession was steep, but the 2009–19 recovery was weak. Post-1980 recoveries averaged 3.2 percent growth. The post-2009 recovery produced only 2.2 percent growth. It was a real recovery, yet the output gap between the former trend and the new trend was never closed. The U.S. economy suffered over $4 trillion of lost wealth based on the difference between the former strong trend and the new weaker trend. That lost wealth was a serious problem for the United States in terms of income inequality and the national debt–to–GDP ratio, even before the New Great Depression. Today the prospect is for even lower growth than the weak post-2009 recovery. The new recovery, far from the 6 percent growth discussed in the example above, may produce only 1.8 percent growth due to excessive government debt and high precautionary personal savings. That's even worse than the 2.2 percent average annual growth in the ten-year expansion before the pandemic. It's another L-shaped recovery, the second in a row. Now the bottom of the L will be even closer to a flat line, and the output gap compared with the long-term trend even greater.

Some causes of this weak growth were discussed above, including a second wave of layoffs, government incentives to delay a return to work, bankruptcies, a collapse of world trade, a growing work-from-home business model, declining labor-force participation, and recursive functions whereby weakness begets weakness in upstream supply chains. Still, there's another factor that may dominate these trends and ensure low growth—that factor is high savings.

A high savings rate sounds like a desirable outcome. In the long run, it is. Savings can translate into investment, which is the source of jobs and higher productivity that lead to economic growth. This assumes the investment is not wasted on white-elephant ghost cities and other unproductive infrastructure, as in China. The United States has ample high-productivity investment opportunities in infrastructure, education, and research, so the prospects are good that U.S. investment can be a key to growth.

The problem is that, although investment has long-term payoffs, it comes at the expense of short-term consumption. The U.S. economy is driven 70 percent by consumption. There's no way to increase investment (for the long run) without killing consumption (in the short run) unless the United States runs higher deficits and borrows more from abroad. Yet U.S. deficits are already at record levels, and foreign nations have their own economic collapses and public deficits to deal with.

Darius Dale, an analyst for market research firm Hedgeye, points out that many of the programs that sustained the economy since March 2020 have expired or will do so in short order. July 15, 2020, was when federal income tax payments (extended from April) were due. September 30, 2020, was when the student loan–forbearance program ended. October 31, 2020, marked the scheduled end of the mortgage-forbearance program. December 31, 2020, was the end of the Payroll Protection Program loan grace period. To the extent that these and other programs are not extended or expanded with more funding, important props will be pulled out from under an already-weak pandemic recovery. This suggests the economy in 2021 will quickly resume the downward spiral that was truncated by government intervention in March–June 2020.

Based on the most rigorous study available, our projections of slow growth for several years are too modest. The best evidence points to slow growth for *thirty years*. A March 2020 study entitled "Longer-Run Economic Consequences of Pandemics," by a Federal Reserve economist and two academics from the University of California, examines the economic impact of pandemics with at least 100,000 deaths, beginning with the Black Death in 1347. The authors' conclusion states, "Significant macroeconomic after-effects of the pandemics persist for about 40 years, with real rates of return substantially depressed." They go on to say, "Pandemics have effects that last for decades. . . . These results are staggering." For context, the COVID-19 pandemic is on track to cause more fatalities than all but four of the fifteen pandemics studied.

Trade-offs between savings and consumption are academic at this point, because Americans have already voted with their wallets. In May 2020, U.S. savings as a percentage of disposable income skyrocketed from 7.5 percent to 33.0 percent. Americans were saving, not spending. This makes sense if you were unemployed and worried about making the next car payment or rent payment. It also makes sense if you are not unemployed yet worry you might be next to get a pink slip. Even if your job and income are secure, you might save more because of the prospect of deflation. In deflation, cash can be your best-performing asset, because the real value of cash goes up as the cost of living goes down.

All of these elements—more layoffs, more bankruptcies, feedback loops, and a spending strike in the form of higher savings—mean the recovery will be slow and unemployment will stay high. There will be no V-shaped recovery. There are no green shoots, despite what you hear from the media. We are in the New Great Depression and will remain so for years.

CHAPTER FOUR

DEBT AND DEFLATION DERAIL RECOVERY

Today, the United States and other advanced countries are experiencing the second wave of an especially powerful twin shock. Taken individually, either the global financial crisis of 2008 or the global pandemic of 2020 would have been enough to change public finances, driving governments to create and borrow money freely. Combined, these two crises are set to transform the spending power of the state. . . . Call it the age of magic money.

—Sebastian Mallaby, *Foreign Affairs* (July/August 2020)

Where are we going? With the SARS-CoV-2 scourge revealed and depression's devastation in almost every home, the focus is on what's next. Individuals, businesses, and communities are reeling from the simultaneous impact of pandemic, lockdown, depression, and riots in major American cities. Resiliency is an American trait, as shown by economic restoration following the Civil War and the Great Depression. Restoration requires hope, leadership, and a set of public policies designed to undo damage, offer direction, and provide a platform on which people and commerce can resume risk taking, rehiring, and hard work. The Civil War was followed by Reconstruction, railroad building, and a sustained period of technological innovation beginning around 1870. The Great Depression was alleviated first by infrastructure spending on projects such as the Grand Coulee Dam (1933–42) and finally by the massive ramp-up of war industries as the United States entered the global conflagration. Recessions and weak growth during demobilization after the Second World War were offset in the 1950s by expanded national defense spending, massive infrastructure projects such as the Eisenhower Interstate Highway System, and a demographic boost from the baby boom. None of these responses were single silver-bullet solutions; they interacted with other policies and larger trends, and they took time. Still, the announcement and implementation of important public-policy approaches had tangible effects in terms of jobs and spending and had more important psychological effects through which confidence was restored and a springboard provided for private-sector investment and entrepreneurship to amplify public policies. This was not a "public-private partnership" in the programmatic sense in which that term is used today. It was an organic, recursive function in which government initiatives prompted private efforts that in turn provided growth and tax revenue to support the government.

What is the public-policy response to the New Great Depression and the pandemic that caused it? In broad terms, there has been a massive monetary-policy response in the form of guarantees, money printing, and surging liquidity where needed. There has been an unparalleled fiscal-policy response involving increased unemployment benefits, soft-money loans to support payrolls, and bailouts of afflicted airlines, hotels, resorts, and other industries badly damaged in the depression. Behind these multitrillion-dollar deficit- and debt-monetization efforts is an ersatz economic mélange called Modern Monetary Theory (MMT), which purports to alleviate concerns about debt sustainability. Until recently, MMT was a fringe view with some support on the far left. Today it is de facto the economic law of the land even if most of the legislators who enshrined MMT have never heard of it.

We examine MMT, monetary policy, and fiscal policy as crisis responses in the sections below. None of these policies accomplishes the goals of ending the depression, recovering lost jobs, and regaining real growth. There are empirically and behaviorally valid reasons why these policies will fail. Finally, we examine the greatest danger of all—deflation—and why seemingly unlimited money printing and spending won't end it. There is a cure for deflation (which we explore in the conclusion), yet that cure is not in the intellectual tool kit of central bankers or legislators today. This phrenic void presages years of low growth; it is one more reason we face a depression and not a mere recession and one more reason investors need to be acutely forward-leaning to avoid lost wealth and lost opportunities.

MMT TO THE RESCUE

The need to spend money in response to the economic shock from the COVID-19 pandemic has moved Modern Monetary Theory from the fringes of economic policy to a place at center stage. Modern Monetary Theorists such as Bard College professor L. Randall Wray and investor Warren Mosler offer a curious blend of progressivism and a pre-Keynesian concept called chartalism. MMT advocates are a small but ascendant clique who offer the world what the world wants most—free money.

The two key institutions, in the view of MMT seers, are the Federal Reserve and the U.S. Treasury. The Fed and the Treasury were created separately and have different governance, yet they work together in myriad ways. The Treasury has an account at the Fed, the Fed buys Treasury debt with printed money, and the Fed remits profits to the Treasury. Yet the two institutions have boundaries respected by economists and policy makers. The Treasury does not create money. Treasury spending is constrained if Congress does not authorize it or if the Fed does not accommodate it with low interest rates and asset purchases.

MMT rejects these constraints. In effect, MMT scholars treat the Treasury and Fed as if they were a single entity. In MMT's model, the Treasury creates money by spending. When the Treasury spends money, it reduces its bank account at the Fed and increases the private-sector bank accounts of citizens or companies that are recipients of the Treasury spending. In this view, private-sector wealth is increased by Treasury spending. The more the Treasury spends, the richer the private sector becomes. The MMT crowd ask rhetorically, "Where would money come from in the first place if the Treasury didn't spend it?"

MMT supporters view money as a bookkeeping exercise initiated by Treasury spending and backed by state power; there is no limit to the amount of money the state can spend. If that's true, there is no social problem, from poverty to infrastructure to education, that cannot be solved with more spending. The country does not get poorer when the Treasury borrows and spends; it gets richer because Treasury spending becomes wealth of the recipients.

Modern Monetary Theory has been manna for those members of Congress looking to increase deficit spending by more in one year than the cumulative national debt of every president combined, from George Washington to Bill Clinton. Congress doesn't mind spending money, yet it needs some sort of intellectual air cover when the projected deficit for a single year is over 20 percent of GDP. Modern Monetary Theory fills the bill, even if it's a scholarly snow job. By the time its real-world deficiencies come to light, the money will be long gone and the American people will be left to pick up the pieces.

Modern Monetary Theory is old wine in new bottles. The old wine consists of the belief that the value of money is created by government dictate and the volume of money is unlimited because government offers citizens no choice but to use their money as payment for taxes. As long as government money is the only medium with which to pay taxes, citizens must acquire that approved form of money to avoid incarceration for tax evasion. It's a closed system with no escape. The new bottles consist of hitching MMT to a wish list of progressive programs such as Medicare for all, free tuition, free child care, and a guaranteed basic income. In years past, these policy proposals were easily derailed by experts who said, "We can't afford it." Today MMT advocates reply, "Yes, we can," with a patina of theoretical respectability. Caught in the middle are legislators who formerly had some intuitive sense that there were limits on deficit spending (even if liberals and conservatives disagreed on what those limits might be) and now see no limits at all, provided spending addresses short-term problems caused by the pandemic and economic depression. Members of Congress who voted for $3 trillion of new deficit spending between March and July 2020 might not have heard of MMT, yet that is what they espoused by their actions.

The brightest advocate for MMT is Professor Stephanie Kelton of Stony Brook University. Her views are encapsulated in her new book, *The Deficit Myth: Modern Monetary Theory and the Birth of the People's Economy* (2020). In Kelton's version of MMT, crumbling infrastructure can be fixed immediately by spending money on improvements. The $1.6 trillion mountain of student-loan debt impeding household formation and turning millennials into debt slaves is remedied with debt forgiveness. Unemployment and underemployment are cured with a guaranteed basic income in the form of a monthly check sent to every American, with no work requirements or other strings attached. These and other government programs can be funded by Treasury expenditures and debt monetization by the Fed.

Kelton is also a portal to the dark side of MMT—the government's monopoly on violence and willingness to use it against citizens who demur at the use of state money. MMT purports to be a twenty-first-century approach to the problems of government finance and economic growth. In fact, MMT advocates embrace the tenets of chartalism advanced almost a century ago by Georg Friedrich Knapp, the father of chartalism, in his work *The State Theory of Money*, published in 1924.

According to Kelton and Knapp, your money is valuable because the state says so. From this reasoning, Kelton and her ilk expand in all directions. If money is what the state says it is, then anything can be money, including gold. Prior to the late twentieth century, most state money was gold. Kelton claims gold was money not because of scarcity or utility but because the state proclaimed it money as a matter of custom more than necessity. Once paper became the object of the proclamation, paper became money and gold fell by the wayside.

Kelton claims that debt and credit are the same thing viewed from different perspectives. If the state transfers dollars to citizens, the state is a debtor because dollars are central-bank liabilities, and citizens are creditors because they accept and hold the debt. This concept that money = debt allows Kelton to create what she calls a "hierarchy of money." Literally anyone can create money in some form by issuing an IOU. It's as if the Federal Reserve expanded its definitions of money supply from M0, M1, and M2 to include M4, M5, M6, and so on. It's all money, all credit, and all debt at the same time.

Kelton is honest about the need for state power to make this system work. She writes, "Only the state, through its power to make and enforce tax laws, can issue promises that its constituents must accept if they are to avoid penalties." She does not explicitly say penalties include property confiscation and imprisonment for nonpayment of taxes, yet that is the unavoidable implication. State power is the root of state money.

It is true that state power can proclaim the kind of money acceptable for payment of taxes. It is true that citizens may regard the declared form of money as money in order to pay taxes and avoid prison. It is true that a central bank and a treasury can work together in a condition called "fiscal dominance" to monetize unlimited government debt and support unlimited government spending. Finally, it is true that government spending goes into someone's pocket and enriches that individual or company by that amount of spending, at least temporarily.

MMT fails not because of what it says but because of what it ignores. The issue is not whether there is a legal limit on money creation but whether there is a psychological limit.

The real source of money status is not state power; it's confidence. If two parties to a transaction have confidence that their medium of exchange is money, and others regard it as such, then that medium *is* money in the wider society. In times past, money consisted of gold, silver, beads, feathers, paper tokens, and diverse badges of confidence.

The difficulty with confidence is that it's fragile, easily lost, and impossible to regain. MMT's great failing is that it takes confidence for granted. Reasons for ignoring confidence range from overreliance on quantitative models to overreliance on state power. As for the former, ignoring psychology because it does not fit neatly into quantitative equilibrium models is no less than willful ignorance. As for the latter, one need only consider the long history of failed states, which today include Venezuela, Somalia, Syria, Yemen, Lebanon, and North Korea. State power is not absolute and it is not permanent.

MMT's other blind spot is velocity or turnover of money. Velocity is scarcely discussed in MMT literature. Only by ignoring velocity can MMT champions such as Kelton and Wray wish away hyperinflation as confidence in state money erodes. The reaction to lost confidence in one form of money is to spend it as fast as possible or acquire another form.

This behavioral adaptation, not money printing, is the real cause of inflation. Confidence and velocity are inversely correlated and together are the Achilles' heel of MMT.

Kelton is undaunted by such concerns. In a June 9, 2020, op-ed in the *New York Times*, she described pandemic-related financial bailouts as follows: "Lawmakers simply voted to pass spending bills, which effectively ordered up trillions of dollars from the government's bank, the Federal Reserve." Such simplification is politically appealing but ignores the behavioral adaptations that accompany excessive debt expansion. Those adaptations, such as higher savings rates and reduced consumption, make the nascent liquidity trap worse, not better.

MMT's intellectual failings will become apparent in the next several years. This could play out as persistent deflation (because MMT policies cannot create growth) or as inflation (as MMT policies destroy confidence in state money). Likely both will emerge: deflation first, followed by inflation.

For now, the importance of MMT is not that it works (it doesn't) but that it provides a cloak of credibility for Congress to spend unlimited amounts and for the Federal Reserve to monetize that spending. Both monetary policy and fiscal policy are in overdrive to "stimulate" the U.S. economy in the face of the New Great Depression. Neither money printing nor spending provides stimulus, for reasons explained in the following sections. The academic lip gloss of MMT does not change that result.

WHY MONETARY POLICY IS NOT STIMULUS

Since 2007, the Fed has piled failure upon failure, which it obscures by making each failure larger than the one before. We're nearing the endgame. To understand why, we need to look at where we've been.

The Fed's response to what became the 2008 global financial crisis began in August 2007 in the aftermath of the failure of two Bear Stearns mortgage-securities hedge funds in late July. The effective federal funds rate (the policy rate targeted by the Fed) fell from 5.26 percent in July to 5.02 percent in August 2007. From there the drop was precipitous, and the Fed funds rate hit 0.15 percent by January 2009. At that point, Fed chair Ben Bernanke had no more interest-rate ammunition and resorted to money printing under the name of "quantitative easing." This came in three waves called QE1, QE2, and QE3. The effect of the money printing was to increase the Fed's balance sheet from $865 billion in August 2007 at the start of the crisis to over $4.52 trillion on January 12, 2015, just after the completion of the QE3 "taper," which had gradually reduced the amount of new money printing to zero. From there, the Fed kept its interest rates at zero and its balance sheet at about $4.5 trillion until the first interest-rate increase on December 16, 2015 (the so-called liftoff). The federal funds target rate increased steadily to 2.50 percent on December 20, 2018. The Fed also started to reduce its balance sheet in November 2017 under a program called "quantitative tightening" or QT. This amounted to destroying base money. The Fed reduced its balance sheet to $3.76 trillion by August 26, 2019, a $760 billion reduction in assets in less than two years. Analysts estimated that every $500 billion reduction in money supply was roughly equivalent to a 1.0 percent increase in interest rates. The combination of real rate hikes and effective rate hikes (through QT) meant the Fed was engaged in an extreme form of monetary tightening in 2015–18 in what was still a weak economy. Of course, the Fed did not understand this due to its deficient forecasting ability.

Both the increase in interest rates starting in 2015 and reduction in the balance sheet starting in 2017 were efforts by the Fed to normalize rates and money supply. The Fed's goal was to push rates to the 4 percent level and reduce assets to around $2.5 trillion to prepare for the next recession. If the Fed could normalize, it would have enough dry powder in the form of potential rate cuts and money-supply increases to fight a recession. The conundrum was whether the Fed could normalize before a recession without *causing* the recession it was preparing to fight. My view was always that the Fed would fail, that there was no exit from zero rates and a bloated balance sheet without causing a recession. The Fed did fail. Stocks plunged almost 20 percent from October 1, 2018, to December 24, 2018 (the infamous Christmas Eve Massacre), in response to the Fed's overtightening.

Fed chair Jay Powell quickly reversed course in late December 2018. Powell first signaled he would not raise rates further (using the code word "patience" in public statements). By March 2019, the Fed signaled rate cuts, and it followed through on July 31, 2019, with the first of three rate cuts that year. The Fed also announced the end of quantitative tightening (QT), a method for reducing the money supply, and began to expand its balance sheet again. This double easing through rate cuts and new money printing was a tonic for the stock market. Stocks rallied strongly before hitting new highs in February 2020, just before the pandemic crash.

This chronology of extreme easing (2007–14) followed by extreme tightening (2015–18) followed by extreme easing again (2019–20) omits a curious shock that emerged in September 2019. The Fed expanded its balance sheet from $3.8 trillion on September 16, 2019, to $4.2 trillion on December 31, 2019. This expansion occurred *before* any economic impact from SARS-CoV-2 and *before* the new depression. What prompted this money printing was a severe liquidity crisis that arose in the U.S. Treasury market in late September. The exact cause was never revealed, although it likely involved the near failure of one or more hedge funds and their lender banks. This narrowly averted crisis was the result of a global shortage of dollars and good collateral (usually U.S. Treasury notes) for secured lending. Put simply, the world was in a dollar-liquidity crisis five months *before* the pandemic and new depression hit home. The pandemic was a force multiplier on what was already a financial crisis, albeit one not well understood by nonspecialists in government bond markets.

This chronology is one long story of the failure of monetary policy in general and of monetarism (described below) in particular. The Fed failed to return the economy to the previous level of growth after 2009. The Fed failed to normalize interest rates or its balance sheet from 2014 to 2020. The Fed failed to sustain its 2 percent inflation target for the past thirteen years and counting. The Fed nearly caused a recession and a stock market crash in late 2018 before abruptly reversing course. The Fed failed to foresee a dollar-liquidity crisis coming in September 2019. Now the Fed has abandoned any pretense of integrity by increasing its balance sheet from $4.2 trillion to $7.2 trillion between March 1 and June 1, 2020. Additional trillions of dollars of balance sheet expansion are expected in 2021. The Fed is capable of only one task—inflating stock market valuations as needed. Stock market investors have taken note and respond accordingly. Pumping up stock markets is not part of the Fed's dual mandate (price stability and maximum employment), yet the Fed is good at it.

The Fed did succeed in keeping the lights on when the market crash hit in February 2020. Providing liquidity in a crisis is the original mission of the Federal Reserve as it was conceived in 1913, its year of creation, in response to the Panic of 1907. Using a combination of money printing, direct investment, direct lending, guarantees, and off-balance-sheet vehicles, the Fed launched the Term Asset-Backed Securities Loan Facility, the Primary Market Corporate Credit Facility, the Payroll Protection Program Liquidity Facility, the Municipal Liquidity Facility, the Main Street Lending Program, the Money Market Mutual Fund Liquidity Facility, and the Commercial Paper Funding Facility. No doubt the Fed will create as many funds and facilities as needed to keep markets liquid and keep the banks open. The difficulty is that none of these programs provides stimulus or creates jobs. None of them will return the economy to trend growth (even the weak 2009–19 trend growth). They will keep hedge funds and banks from failing, and they will keep trading markets from freezing up in the short run. Yet these programs are not a source of jobs or growth.

The reason for this world-historic litany of failure by the Fed can be reduced to one word—"velocity"—the turnover of money. To understand why, a detour through the theory of monetarism is needed.

Monetarism is an economic theory closely associated with Milton Friedman, winner of the Nobel Prize in economics in 1976. Its basic idea is that changes in money supply are the most important cause of changes in GDP. These GDP changes, measured in dollars, are broken into two parts: a real component, which produces actual gains, and an inflationary component, which is illusory. The real plus the inflationary equals the nominal increase, measured in total dollars.

Friedman's contribution was to show that increasing money supply in order to increase output would work only up to a certain point; beyond that, nominal gains would be inflationary. In effect, the Fed could print money to get nominal growth, yet there would be a limit to how much real growth could result.

A monetarist attempting to fine-tune monetary policy says that if real growth is capped at 4 percent, the ideal policy is one in which money supply grows at 4 percent, velocity is constant, and the price level is constant. This produces maximum real growth and zero inflation. It's all fairly simple, as long as the velocity of money is constant.

What if velocity is not constant?

It turns out that velocity is not constant, contrary to Friedman's thesis. Velocity is like a joker in the deck. It's the factor the Fed cannot control. Velocity is psychological: It depends on how an individual feels about her economic prospects. Velocity cannot be controlled by the Fed's printing press. That's the fatal flaw in monetarism as a policy tool. Velocity is a behavioral phenomenon, and a powerful one.

Velocity of M2 (a broad definition of money supply) peaked at 2.2 in 1997. This means that each dollar of M2 supported $2.20 of nominal GDP. Velocity has been declining precipitously ever since. It fell to 2.0 in 2006, just before the global financial crisis, and then crashed to 1.7 in mid-2009 as the crisis hit bottom. The velocity crash did not stop with the market crash. Velocity continued to fall to 1.43 by late 2017, despite the Fed's money printing and zero-rate policy (2008–15). Even before the new pandemic-related crash, velocity fell to 1.37 in early 2020. It can be expected to fall even further as the New Great Depression drags on.

When consumers pay down debt and increase savings instead of spending, velocity drops, as does GDP, unless the Fed increases the money supply. The Fed is printing money prodigiously to maintain nominal GDP in the face of declining velocity, a problem it has not faced since the 1930s. As velocity approaches zero, the economy approaches zero as well. Money printing is impotent: $7 trillion times zero equals zero. If the money-expansion mechanism is broken because banks will not lend, and velocity is declining because of consumer fears, then it's impossible for the economy to grow. There is no economy without velocity.

This brings us to the crux. The factors the Fed can control, such as base money, are not growing fast enough to revive the economy and decrease unemployment. The factors that the Fed needs to accelerate are bank lending and velocity in the form of spending. Spending is driven by the psychology of lenders and consumers, essentially a behavioral phenomenon. The Fed has forgotten (if it ever knew) the art of changing expectations about inflation, which is the key to changing consumer behavior and driving growth. It has almost nothing to do with money supply, contrary to the nostrums of monetarists and Austrian School economists.

Two U.S. presidents since the turn of the twentieth century have been successful at radically changing consumer expectations about inflation. Both used the same technique. One president did it by design, the other by accident. One saved the U.S. economy; the other nearly destroyed it. Causing inflation is like letting a genie out of the bottle; the result can be good or bad. Without an increase in inflation caused by increased velocity, there is no hope of avoiding a deflationary abyss and worsening depression. The stories of the presidents who did increase velocity and how it can be done again are told in the conclusion.

WHY FISCAL POLICY IS NOT STIMULUS

Congress authorized more deficit spending in 2020 than in the last eight years combined. Congress will add more to the national debt in 2020–21 than the cumulative debt of all presidents from George Washington to Bill Clinton. This spending saturnalia includes $26 billion for virus testing; $126 billion for administrative costs of programs; $217 billion in direct aid to state and local governments; $312 billion for public health; $513 billion in tax breaks for business; $532 billion to bail out major corporations; $784 billion in aid to individuals as unemployment benefits, paid leave, and direct cash payments; and $810 billion for small business under the Payroll Protection Program. This comes on top of a baseline budget deficit of $1 trillion. Combining the baseline deficit and approved spending brings the total deficit for 2020 to $4.3 trillion. That added debt will increase the U.S. debt-to-GDP ratio to 130 percent. That's the highest in U.S. history and puts the United States in the same superdebtor's league as Japan, Greece, Italy, and Lebanon.

There's no doubt about the amount of deficit spending and its impact on critical debt ratios. There's little debate about the necessity for this spending to keep the economy from spiraling into an even deeper depression than the one we are now witnessing. Yet spending is not "stimulus." Congress is spending money as a temporary bridge until growth is revived, but such spending alone will not deliver growth. The reason lies in both classic economic analysis by John Maynard Keynes and recent analysis by economists Carmen Reinhart and Kenneth Rogoff that defines the limits of what a Keynesian approach can do.

The idea that deficit spending can stimulate an otherwise stalled economy dates to John Maynard Keynes and his classic work *The General Theory of Employment, Interest, and Money* (1936). Keynes's idea was straightforward. He considered output a function of what he called aggregate demand. This is usually driven by business and consumer demand. At times, this demand was lacking because depressionary conditions or deflation drove consumers into a liquidity trap. In this condition, consumers preferred to save rather than spend, both because prices were falling and because the value of cash was going up. In those conditions, it's smart to defer buying (since prices will be cheaper later) and increase savings (since the real value of cash is going up). Keynes's solution to the liquidity trap was to have governments step in with government spending to replace individual spending. Deficits were a perfectly acceptable way to do this, in order to break the back of deflation and revive what Keynes called "animal spirits."

Keynes went further and said that each dollar of government spending could produce more than one dollar of growth. When the government spent money (or gave it away), the recipient would spend it on goods or services. Those providers of goods and services would, in turn, pay their wholesalers and suppliers, which would increase the velocity of money. Depending on the exact economic conditions, it might be possible to generate $1.30 of nominal GDP for each $1.00 of deficit spending. This was the famous Keynesian multiplier. To some extent the deficit would pay for itself in increased output and increased taxes.

In practice, Keynes's theory was not a general theory but a special theory. It would work only in limited conditions. It worked when the economy started in a depression or in the early stages of a recovery. It worked when the initial level of government debt was low and sustainable. In worked in conditions of deflation and a true liquidity trap. Keynes was not an ideologue; he was a consummate pragmatist. His prescription was the right one for the 1930s. Unfortunately, his ideas were grossly distorted after his death by Paul Samuelson and his followers at MIT and other centers of economic thought. Keynes's limited solution was turned into an all-purpose prescription that deficits can be used to promote growth at all times and in all places (provided the spending is aimed at social goals approved by the academic elites). MMT is the reductio ad absurdum of what came from MIT. The belief that deficit spending of any quantity at any time produces more growth than the amount spent is what lies behind the claim of "stimulus" in the congressional frenzy of trillion-dollar deficits now under way. This is a false belief.

In fact, America and the world are inching closer to what Carmen Reinhart and Ken Rogoff describe as an indeterminate yet real point where an ever-increasing debt burden triggers creditor revulsion, forcing a debtor nation into austerity, outright default, or sky-high interest rates.

The creditor-revulsion point, where more debt does not produce commensurate growth due to lost confidence in the debtor's currency, is reached as follows: A country begins with a manageable debt-to-GDP ratio, commonly defined as less than 60 percent. In a search for economic growth, perhaps to emerge from a recession or simply to buy votes, policy makers start down a path of increased borrowing and deficit spending. Initially, results can be positive. Some Keynesian multiplier may apply, especially if the economy has underutilized industrial and labor-force capacity and assuming the borrowed money is used wisely, in ways that have positive payoffs.

Over time, the debt-to-GDP ratio pushes into a range of 70 to 80 percent. Political constituencies develop around increased spending. The spending itself becomes less productive; more is spent on current consumption in the form of entitlements, benefits, and less-fruitful public amenities, community organizations, and public-employee unions. The law of diminishing marginal returns starts to bind. Yet the public's appetite for deficit spending and public goods is insatiable. The debt-to-GDP ratio eventually pushes past 90 percent.

The Reinhart and Rogoff research reveals that a 90 percent debt-to-GDP ratio is not just more of the same; rather it's what physicists call a critical threshold at which a phase transition occurs. The first effect is that the Keynesian multiplier falls below one. A dollar of debt and spending produces less than a dollar of growth. No net growth is created by added debt, while interest on the debt increases the debt-to-GDP ratio on its own. Today pandemic-related debt creation is not incremental; it's exponential relative to prior deficits. And it comes at a time when the debt-to-GDP ratio is already well past the Reinhart-Rogoff 90 percent red line.

Creditors grow anxious while continuing to buy more debt in a vain hope that policy makers will reverse course or growth will spontaneously emerge to lower the ratio. This doesn't happen. Society is addicted to debt, and the addiction consumes the addict. The United States is the best credit market in the world and borrows in a currency it prints; for that reason alone, it can pursue an unsustainable debt dynamic longer than other nations. Yet history shows there is always a limit.

Those considering endgame scenarios agree a U.S. default (whether by nonpayment or inflation) is not imminent. This does not mean all is well. The salience of the Reinhart-Rogoff research is not the imminence of default but the weight of structural headwinds to growth. Of particular importance to the United States is the Reinhart-Rogoff paper "Debt and Growth Revisited" (2010). The authors' main conclusion is that for debt-to-GDP ratios above 90 percent, "median growth rates fall by 1%, and average growth falls considerably more." Importantly, Reinhart and Rogoff emphasize "the importance of nonlinearities in the debt-growth link." For debt-to-equity ratios below 90 percent, "there is no systematic relationship between debt and growth." Put differently, the relationship between debt and growth is not strong at lower ratios; other factors, including tax, monetary, and trade policies, all guide growth. Once the 90 percent threshold is crossed, debt is the dominant factor. Above 90 percent debt-to-GDP, an economy goes through the looking glass into a new world of negative marginal returns on debt, slow growth, and eventual default through nonpayment, inflation, or renegotiation.

This point of default is sure to arrive, yet it will be preceded by a long period of weak growth, stagnant wages, rising income inequality, and social discord—a phase where dissatisfaction is widespread, yet no denouement occurs. Other respected research reaches the same conclusion. Reinhart and Rogoff may have led the way in this field, but they are not out on a limb. Evidence is accumulating that developed economies, in particular the United States, are on dangerous ground and possibly past a point of no return.

The end point is a rapid collapse of confidence in U.S. debt and the U.S. dollar. This means higher interest rates to attract investor dollars to continue financing the deficits. Of course, higher interest rates mean larger deficits, which makes the debt situation worse. Or the Fed could monetize the debt (as the MMT followers would have it), yet that's just another path to lost confidence. You cannot borrow your way out of a debt trap and you cannot print your way out of a liquidity trap. The result is another twenty years of slow growth, austerity, financial repression (where interest rates are held below the rate of inflation to gradually extinguish the real value of debt), and an expanding wealth gap. The next two decades of U.S. growth would look like the last three decades in Japan. Not a collapse, just a long, slow stagnation—another name for depression.

DEFLATIONARY DEAD END

Modern Monetary Theory is an intellectual sham that celebrates the coercive power of the state and fails to credit the importance of confidence in the operation of a monetary system. Monetary policy fails because it ignores the behavioral root of velocity, relying on money creation and not comprehending why people refuse to spend money even when it's offered up by the truckload. Fiscal policy fails because debt is so high already that citizens adapt their behavior to a world where default, inflation, or higher taxes are the only ways out. Those three paths have one factor in common—they augur more savings and less spending in preparation for the economic endgame. Over these three sinking ships hangs the specter of deflation.

The New Great Depression will produce powerful and persistent deflation, a result the U.S. Treasury and Federal Reserve fear more than any other economic outcome. Deflation is the most feared outcome because it makes the debt burden worse, yet it's the most likely outcome because of the self-fulfilling liquidity trap.

Deflation means a decline in price levels for goods and services. Lower prices allow for a higher living standard even when wages are constant, because consumer goods cost less. This seems a desirable outcome, based on advances in technology and productivity that result in certain products dropping in price over time. Why, then, is the Federal Reserve so fearful of deflation that it resorts to extraordinary policy measures intended to cause inflation? There are three reasons for this fear.

The first is deflation's impact on government debt. Debt's real value may fluctuate based on inflation or deflation, yet the nominal value of a debt is fixed by contract. If one borrows $1 million, then one must repay $1 million plus interest, regardless of whether the real value of $1 million is greater or less due to deflation or inflation. U.S. debt is at a point where no feasible combination of real growth and taxes will finance repayment of the real amount owed. If the Fed can cause inflation—slowly at first, to create money illusion, and then more rapidly—the debt will be manageable because it will be repaid in less-valuable nominal dollars. In deflation, the opposite occurs: The real value of debt increases, making repayment more difficult.

The second problem with deflation is its impact on the debt-to-GDP ratio. This ratio is the debt amount divided by the amount of GDP expressed in nominal terms. Debt is continually increasing in nominal terms because of continuing budget deficits that require new financing and associated interest payments. In the debt-to-GDP ratio, when the debt numerator expands and the GDP denominator shrinks, as is happening today, the ratio increases. The impact of sky-high debt-to-GDP ratios is a loss of confidence, higher interest rates, worse deficits because of the higher interest rates, and finally an outright default on the debt through either nonpayment or inflation.

The third deflation concern has to do with the health of the banking system and systemic risk. Deflation increases money's real value and therefore increases the real value of lenders' claims on debtors. This would seem to favor lenders over debtors, and initially it does. Yet as deflation progresses, the weight of the debt becomes too great, and debtors default. This puts the losses on the bank lenders. The government prefers inflation, because it props up the banking system by keeping debtors solvent.

In summary, the Federal Reserve prefers inflation because it erases government debt, reduces the debt-to-GDP ratio, and props up the banks. Deflation may help consumers and workers, yet it hurts the Treasury and the banks and is firmly opposed by the Fed. From the Fed's perspective, aiding the economy and reducing unemployment are incidental by-products of the drive to inflate. The consequence of these deflationary dynamics is that the government must have inflation, *and the Fed must cause it*. The irony is that the Fed does not know how.

The New Great Depression will be characterized by powerful deflation, at least initially. This deflation will be the result of greatly increased savings, reduced spending, and falling money velocity. Lower prices will beget more saving, which will beget lower prices, and so on, in a classic liquidity trap and deflationary spiral. Workers who have lost their jobs, businesses that have shut their doors, and others who fear they will be next to suffer the same fate will be in no mood to borrow or spend. Deflation is the immovable object that defeats the combined forces of easy money and big deficits. Neither the Fed nor Congress will achieve their stimulus goals until they defeat deflation, an enemy they have not faced in such virulent form since the 1930s.

CHAPTER FIVE

CIVILIZATION'S THIN VENEER

The stranger swung into his saddle beside her, leaned far towards
her and regarded her without meaning, the blank still stare of
mindless malice that makes no threats and can bide its time. . . .
The stranger rode beside her, easily, lightly, his reins loose in his
half-closed hand, straight and elegant in dark shabby garments
that flapped upon his bones; his pale face smiled in an evil trance,
he did not glance at her. Ah, I have seen this fellow before, I know
this man if I could place him. He is no stranger to me.

—**Katherine Anne Porter,** *Pale Horse, Pale Rider* **(1939)**

Katherine Anne Porter was one of the finest American writers of the
twentieth century. She was critically acclaimed for her short stories
and novels yet had limited financial success until the publication of her
best-known work, the 1962 novel *Ship of Fools*, based on a cruise she took
from Veracruz, Mexico, to Germany in 1931. The novel was adapted into
a screenplay and produced as a film in 1965 starring Vivien Leigh. The
film was nominated for eight Academy Awards and won two, for art

direction and cinematography. In 1966 Porter was awarded the Pulitzer Prize and the National Book Award upon publication of *The Collected Stories of Katherine Anne Porter.*

Among her earlier works, still critically acclaimed, is a collection of three short novels in a single volume called *Pale Horse, Pale Rider*, including the eponymous novel, published in 1939. The title is a reference to the Four Horsemen of the Apocalypse described in Revelation 6:8: "I looked, and there was a pale green horse. Its rider was named Death, and Hades accompanied him. They were given authority over a quarter of the earth, to kill with sword, famine and plague."

Porter herself had faced death as a result of plague—she was a survivor of the Spanish flu pandemic of 1918. Porter nearly died from Spanish flu; she experienced hallucinations and delirium in the course of the disease. Her recovery in a hospital took months, and she was weak and bald upon discharge. Her black hair grew back white and remained white the rest of her life.

The novel *Pale Horse, Pale Rider* is a love story of a couple in their early twenties, a newspaper writer, Miranda, and Adam, a soldier about to go France to fight in the First World War. Miranda is infected with the flu virus. She progresses through the usual symptoms—cough, fever, difficulty breathing—before reaching an acute stage of high fever and delirium. She is nursed, first by Adam in her room, then by a professional nurse, Miss Tanner, after being moved to a hospital. In Miranda's delirious state, the line between reality and dreams is gone. She has visions of heaven and hell. Doctors are executioners and patients are condemned prisoners. Porter writes:

The two living men lifted a mattress standing hunched against the wall, spread it tenderly and exactly over the dead man. . . . It had been an entrancing and leisurely spectacle, but now it was over. A pallid white fog rose in their wake insinuatingly and floated before Miranda's eyes, a fog in which was concealed all terror and all weariness, all the wrung faces and twisted backs and broken feet of abused, outraged living things, all the shapes of their confused pain and their estranged hearts; the fog might part at any moment and loose the horde of human torments. She put up her hands and said, Not yet, not yet, but it was too late. The fog parted and two executioners, white clad, moved towards her.

Two traits set Porter apart from others of her generation who lived through the Spanish flu. The first was the quality of her writing, which still moves us today and brings us closer to the flu victims in ways no scientific study can. The second was that she was practically alone in writing about it. The best estimates are that as many as 100 million died from the Spanish flu. More than 500 million people were infected, about one third of the human population in 1918. The flu was especially lethal for those in their twenties and thirties, in contrast to most pandemics, which are more lethal for the very young and very old. More people died from the Spanish flu than died in the First World War. The Spanish flu is ranked as the second-deadliest pandemic in history, after the fourteenth-century Black Death.

One might have expected that a natural catastrophe of that magnitude, where almost everyone either contracted the disease or knew someone who did, or even knew a fatality, would have occasioned an outpouring of literature, art, or commentary on the experience itself or its impact on society. That never happened. Great writers like Ernest Hemingway, F. Scott Fitzgerald, William Faulkner, and John Dos Passos, all of whom were in their early-to-midtwenties in 1918, never mentioned the flu in their writings (although Fitzgerald had a mild case and Hemingway's girlfriend was a nurse to flu victims). Some oblique references appear in D. H. Lawrence's *Lady Chatterley's Lover* and in T. S. Eliot's poetry, yet nothing explicit. Katherine Anne Porter wrote brilliantly and explicitly about the flu. Still, she was almost alone.

Reticence, almost silence, on the part of artists and writers points to a broader phenomenon—everyday survivors rarely spoke of the Spanish flu either. People remembered deceased loved ones and carried their own images of overcrowded wards, dead bodies piled high, and mass graves—yet they rarely discussed their experiences. The flu was not only deadly but also induced a kind of silence, a collective amnesia, as if it had never happened. Life went on; discussion of the Spanish flu did not.

Several explanations have been put forward to throw light upon this generational silence about the second-worst pandemic ever. The first is that the most lethal waves came during the critical last six months of the First World War. The wartime experience and casualties were so horrific it's almost as if the pandemic seemed a sideshow. Of course, it was not. Still, there's only so much horror the mind can process, and it may have been difficult to process flu casualties on top of war casualties. Yet this view does not carry weight in places like India, West Africa, and South America, which were removed from the war zone yet suffered terribly from the flu.

Another factor, confined mainly to Europe, the United States, and Canada, was that wartime censorship severely limited the ability to discuss the pandemic candidly, because it was deemed bad for morale. Reporters and others were routinely arrested and charged with sedition for writing articles that even mentioned wartime hardships or battlefield reverses. The flu was off-limits as a topic. Citizens knew what was going on when they saw bodies piled in the streets or taken away in wagons—without coffins because there were none. Spouses slept with deceased spouses because there was nowhere to take the bodies and nowhere else to sleep. The horror was all around them, yet they could not discuss it openly. That draconian lid on discourse may simply have carried over to the postwar world.

Finally, there is a view, put forward by authors Laura Spinney and Catharine Arnold in their books on the Spanish flu, that the influence of influenza *was* profound but emerged in hidden, even subconscious ways. Novelists John Steinbeck, Mary McCarthy, and Dashiell Hammett all survived the Spanish flu. Arnold writes that "Steinbeck's perspective was forever changed by the experience." She notes that another author, Thomas Wolfe, "left a spellbinding and compelling account of his brother's death from Spanish Flu in his most famous novel, *Look Homeward, Angel.*" Spinney sees the isolation of the flu victim in the demeanor of private detective Sam Spade from Hammett's *The Maltese Falcon.* Spinney points out that even if Spanish flu was not mentioned explicitly, disease and the dysfunction it caused played a large role in literature in the 1920s, particularly in works by Virginia Woolf, James Joyce, and Eugene O'Neill.

Literary and artistic criticism point to the conclusion that the Spanish flu did have a huge influence on culture and society after 1920, yet that influence was hidden, oblique, and mostly did not mention the flu by name. The pandemic experience was seared in the subconscious and emerged indirectly, yet it was there.

This leads to the most underappreciated and least understood facet of the 1918 flu pandemic, with outsized relevance for our own recovery from COVID-19 and the new depression. This involves the impact of viruses on the brain and central nervous system.

Author John M. Barry provides an extensive overview of eyewitness accounts, medical reports, journal articles, and anecdotal evidence, all pointing to the fact that the Spanish flu had a profoundly negative effect on cognition and mental health in many of its victims. Delirium was not uncommon in victims at the height of the infection in the midst of high fever, reduced oxygen flow to the organs, and dehydration. Barry points to evidence that mental illness lasted long after the fever was gone and patients had ostensibly "recovered."

Barry offers excerpts from a wide variety of clinical observations contained in contemporary medical journals and archives:

From Britain: ". . . profound mental inertia with intense physical prostration. Delirium has been very common. . . . It has varied from mere confusion of ideas through all grades of intensity up to maniacal excitement."

From Italy: ". . . influenza psychoses of the acute period . . . as a rule subside in two or three weeks. The psychosis, however, may pass into a state of mental collapse, with stupor which may persist and become actual dementia. In other cases . . . depression and restlessness . . . to [which] can be attributed the large number of suicides during the pandemic of influenza."

From France: ". . . frequent and serious mental disturbances during convalescence from and as a result of influenza . . . The mental disturbances sometimes took on the form of acute delirium with agitation, violence, fear and erotic excitation and at other times was of a depressive nature . . . fear of persecution."

Barry extends his analysis to include President Woodrow Wilson's actions at the 1919 Versailles Peace Conference, which negotiated a treaty to end the First World War. Wilson adamantly opposed harsh reparations on Germany in the early negotiations in February and March 1919. Wilson was then infected with the Spanish flu during a third wave in April 1919 and suffered a severe case. While he was still recovering, his aides noticed a change of attitude, including some paranoia and loss of his former quick grasp of details. Wilson suddenly agreed to French president Georges Clemenceau's demands for ruinous reparations and assigning all responsibility for the war to Germany. Historians concur that the hard peace imposed on Germany in 1919 was a contributing factor to the rise of Adolf Hitler and the National Socialist German Workers' Party in the 1920s and the outbreak of the Second World War in 1939. It's too much to blame Hitler on the Spanish flu. Still, the evidence suggests some linkage between the virus and Wilson's impaired mental health and at least certain outcomes that contributed to another war.

Famed psychiatrist Karl Menninger published an article in the *American Journal of Psychiatry* in 1924 titled "Influenza and Schizophrenia." In his article, Menninger wrote, "Of the psychoses appearing in close conjunction with influenza, as observed during the 1918 pandemic, the schizophrenic syndrome was by far the most frequent." Laura Spinney cites the case of heiress Nancy Cunard, "who caught the flu in early 1919, developed pneumonia, and was dogged by depression throughout her long convalescence."

These and other sources make clear that the deleterious mental-health legacy of Spanish flu was lengthy and pervasive. In many cases that dysfunction emerged violently through murder, suicide, and domestic abuse. In other cases it persisted silently as depression, personality changes, or cognitive confusion. Even in its mildest form the flu conjured a darker more fatalistic muse expressed in writing, film, and painting, although it was not usually mentioned by name. The end of the Spanish flu, which outlasted the First World War, was a prelude to seventy years of turbulence through the Great Depression, the Second World War, the Holocaust, the advent of nuclear weapons, the Cold War, and crises in between. The legacy of the Spanish flu was a century of chaos.

Now, a century later, as we cope with COVID-19, are we facing a new legacy of anger, bitterness, and social disorder? Will the pandemic response of economic lockdown, something that was not done except in limited circumstances during the Spanish flu, cause its own trauma that impedes an economic recovery or makes one impossible? These questions have no definitive medical answer at this stage, yet as with Spanish flu, anecdotal evidence is disturbing. Any resulting dysfunction may be long lasting.

The mental-health damage from COVID-19 takes two forms, as was also true of the Spanish flu. The first is cognitive impairment caused by physical penetration of the central nervous system by the virus. The second is behavioral dysfunction caused by quarantine, isolation, and the psychosocial effects of the commercial lockdown. We consider these consequences separately.

There is preliminary clinical evidence that COVID-19 can cause serious neurological damage, in addition to the obvious damage to the lungs and other organs that has been widely reported. On March 31, 2020, the scientific journal *Radiology* published a study reporting the first case of "acute necrotizing hemorrhagic encephalopathy," a rare condition, that was associated with COVID-19. This condition is a dangerous and potentially lethal inflammation of the brain characterized by seizures and cognitive struggles. The study reports that the patient, a "female airline worker in her late fifties," presented "cough, fever, and altered mental status."

The magazine *Psychology Today* published an article by Dr. Eugene Rubin summarizing mental health issues associated with COVID-19 and calling upon neurological professionals to undertake research to stay ahead of potential cognitive dysfunctions arising from the pandemic. Rubin wrote, "COVID-19 can affect the central nervous system (CNS) in addition to causing the respiratory and other symptoms described widely in the news media. Acute neurobehavioral symptoms are reported by at least a third of infected individuals and include dizziness, headaches, . . . loss of taste and smell, and impaired thinking."

In an ominous echo of the Spanish flu aftermath, Rubin also warned,

"In addition, there are psychiatric symptoms that are not directly related to the virus, but to the consequences of the pandemic itself. How prevalent will symptoms of post-traumatic stress disorder be among frontline healthcare professionals? How much of an upsurge in anxiety disorders, depression, and substance use disorders will occur as a consequence of psychosocial stress, ongoing fear, social isolation, bereavement, job loss, financial insecurity, and loss of purpose?"

Indeed, the social stress and behavioral dysfunction anticipated by Rubin are already appearing. The Recovery Village, an established addiction treatment and rehabilitation network, reported survey results on May 29, 2020, that showed a 55 percent increase in alcohol consumption and a 36 percent increase in illegal drug use in the month prior to the survey. The survey also showed alcohol consumption rose 67 percent in the same time period in states most severely affected by the pandemic (New York, New Jersey, Massachusetts, Rhode Island, and Connecticut). The survey showed 53 percent of those using drugs or alcohol "were trying to cope with stress," and 32 percent "were trying to cope with mental health symptoms, such as anxiety or depression." The report concluded, "there's expected to be a rise in substance abuse throughout the pandemic and increased rates of addiction afterward due to the stress of isolation, boredom, decreased access to recovery resources and unemployment."

The journal *Brain, Behavior, & Immunity—Health* published a peer-reviewed article that warned:

> COVID-19 along with the mitigation strategies being used to address the virus pose significant threats to our individual and collective mental health. . . . The causes of mental health effects in the context of COVID-19 are multifactorial and likely include biological, behavioral, and environmental determinants. We argue

that the COVID-19 crisis significantly threatens our basic human need for human connection, which might serve as a crucial environmental factor that could underlie the overall insult to our mental health. Furthermore, "brain styles" . . . that are informed by a neural taxonomy, might interact with the universal threat to our need for human connection to explain the mental health consequences of COVID-19. . . .

The COVID-19 pandemic is, by definition, a significant threat to humanity. The pandemic is straining our healthcare and economic systems in ways that are significant and obvious. Beyond these domains, COVID-19 poses a profound threat to our most basic human motivations, especially human connection.

The article goes on to describe a long-standing body of psychological research that demonstrates the human need for connection and community. The recent combination of quarantines, self-isolation, economic lockdowns, and simple fear have eroded and in some cases destroyed that needed sense of community. The article points out that "this unprecedented level of physical isolation is incompatible with our basic human instincts and motivations." One detrimental aspect of this is that "an internal sense of control may be difficult" and victims are "more likely to experience social friction." Other deleterious psychological effects are highlighted in the study. The common thread is that lockdown and quarantine produce enormous stress and antisocial reactions, including depression, suicide, and "impaired functioning in social domains."

Christine Vestal, writing for the Pew Charitable Trusts, reports:

Nationwide, mental health call and text centers . . . offer an early picture of how Americans are coping with the coronavirus pandemic.

. . . Crisis centers are reporting 30% to 40% increases in the number of people seeking help. . . .

. . . Mental health experts predict an avalanche of mental health needs as the pandemic progress.

Ultimately, the psychological impact of the pandemic will harm far more people than the virus itself. And the widespread emotional trauma it's evoking will be long lasting, experts say. Already, more than 4 in 10 Americans say that stress related to the pandemic has had a negative impact on their mental health . . .

"There's no doubt that the coronavirus pandemic will be the most psychologically toxic disaster in anyone's lifetime," said George Everly, who teaches . . . at the Johns Hopkins Bloomberg School of Public Health.

A growing body of research reports results consistent with those described above. While still in its early stages, what medical studies (and voluminous anecdotal evidence) reveal are distinct neurological and mental health problems emerging from the COVID-19 pandemic. The first relates to invasion of the brain tissue by the virus, with complications ranging from severe inflammation and death to more mild yet still serious disorientation and cognitive impairment. These conditions are comparable to those resulting from acute infections of the Spanish flu.

The second category is not limited to those infected by the virus; it applies to infected and uninfected alike. This has to do with antisocial and sometimes violent behavior, as well as depression and anxiety resulting from the *response* to the pandemic. This mental dysfunction is the bitter fruit of quarantine, self-isolation, and mandatory lockdown. Once people are cut off from normal social intercourse, conversation, and visits with friends and family, they do not simply bide their time. They withdraw. They fill the time that would otherwise be taken up by quotidian yet socially engaging tasks with fear, delusions, and anger at conditions beyond their control. That's bad enough, yet when the anger is weaponized and aimed at passersby (and perhaps returned in kind), then the stage is set for a broader breakdown of social order.

Direct neurological impairment from SARS-CoV-2 infection is a serious issue that is gaining the attention of scientists. Still, it is unlikely to have anywhere near the impact on society as a similar impairment during the Spanish flu. That's simply a matter of numbers. The Spanish flu infected over 500 million people and killed as many as 100 million. SARS-CoV-2 had infected over 32 million as of October 1, 2020 (the actual number is larger because of a lack of testing), and killed over one million worldwide. Every death is a tragedy and every case of neurological damage deserves attention. Yet the direct viral impact of SARS-CoV-2 is simply a small fraction (less than 10 percent) of those infected with influenza in 1918–19.

The opposite applies when it comes to behavioral effects on the greater numbers who were affected by the COVID-19 lockdown and economic dislocation even if they were not infected. That number includes practically every man, woman, and child in the United States—330 million people—and billions more around the world. This lockdown breakdown syndrome will have vast consequences for society and the economy—indeed, those consequences are emerging daily.

Certain psychological burdens imposed on individuals were not clinical in the sense that a doctor would identify syndromes or conditions, but they were no less damaging in their effects on overall well-being. The reality of life during a pandemic took its toll on millions, whether they contracted the virus or not.

Maryam Zadeh, proprietor of a fitness studio in Brooklyn near the epicenter of the highest fatality count in the world, recalls seeing a fine ash that filled the air and dusted cars outside her Union Street gym in

April, at the height of outbreak. She shuddered at the sudden realization that the ashes were human remains emitted from the nearby Greenwood Heights crematorium. Zadeh saw hearses lined up in the street in front of the South Brooklyn Casket Company, in business on Union Street in Gowanus since 1931. The hearse drivers had come to pick up caskets curbside because the funeral homes had none and there was nowhere else to put the dead. Seamstresses were stitching coffin linings, and craftsmen were attaching handles to the coffins on the street even as they were being loaded onto the hearses, because there was no time to spare in moving virus victims to burial or cremation. Zadeh also recalls a neighbor who died from the virus in a stairwell. Residents in the victim's building were told by officials to put the body in a bathroom with the window open overnight until the deceased could be retrieved the next day. Zadeh's experiences on the front lines of infection were akin to what one sees and hears in a war zone. Indeed, Brooklyn, and the world, were at war with a virus. Such experiences stay with you for a lifetime, even as the virus itself fades into the past.

The virus has no politics; as discussed above, it's not clear to scientists that a virus is even alive. The mental-health effects described in scientific and anecdotal evidence to date, including depression, anxiety, loss of social skills, and some tendency toward violence, apply to state agents such as politicians and police, as well as citizens, shopkeepers, and protesters alike. No one of any political persuasion is immune. That's important because in a polarized society, the tendency is to single out bad actions of the "other side" and downplay the antisocial acts of those whom one supports. Antisocial behavior has political ramifications, yet the behavioral aftermath of COVID-19 is not political; it's clinical and epidemic.

Examples are legion.

On May 5, 2020, a Dallas salon owner, Shelley Luther, was sentenced to seven days in jail and a fine of $500 per day by a Dallas judge on a contempt of court charge for the crime of cutting hair. She was allegedly in violation of a lockdown order, which itself was of dubious legality. Local police could have presented her with a noncriminal citation and a nominal $100 fee (something like a parking ticket), but the allegations were escalated both by the police and the judge. Luther's real crime, according to the record, was her refusal to "apologize" to the court and admit her actions were "selfish." Luther famously replied, "Feeding my kids is not selfish." The incident was widely publicized; Luther became a folk hero while the judge was ridiculed. Still, it seems likely that both Luther's knowing defiance and the judge's overreaction had their roots in the same anxiety and antisocial attitude induced by the lockdown.

A similar scenario played out in Maine, where Rick Savage, the owner of a popular brewpub in the town of Bethel, reopened his establishment in defiance of Governor Janet Mills's lockdown orders. Savage also addressed a public rally on May 3, 2020, at the statehouse in Augusta, urging other state residents to reopen their doors. Maine retaliated by revoking Savage's health license—in effect depriving him of his property and livelihood. Maine's action was probably unconstitutional under the Fourteenth Amendment to the U.S. Constitution; litigation is pending. As in the Luther case in Dallas, the state could have slapped Savage with a citation and a small fine. Instead they set out to destroy his business as an example to the rest. Again, both the citizen and the state were acting out anxiety caused by the pandemic and the economic collapse. Taking political sides does not advance the analysis. Understanding the disease does.

As the lockdown progressed, so did the anger and threats of violence from both opponents of the lockdown and police sent to enforce it. On April 30, 2020, hundreds of protesters, some armed with semiautomatic rifles, gathered at the state capitol building in Lansing, Michigan, to demonstrate their opposition to Governor Gretchen Whitmer's strict lockdown edicts. Some armed protesters entered the gallery of the senate chamber. A similar protest with armed participants took place in Lansing on May 14, 2020.

On May 15, 2020, Lindsey Graham, owner of the Glamour Salon in Salem, Oregon, held a press conference to describe her efforts to reopen her salon contrary to Governor Kate Brown's lockdown orders. Oregon's Occupational Safety and Health Administration imposed a $14,000 fine on the salon. The state's licensing board threatened to revoke the individual licenses of twenty-three stylists associated with the salon, which would prevent them from working anywhere in the state. The legal assault didn't stop there. On May 7, Graham's house was raided by Child Protective Services. Its agents ransacked her house and interrogated her child without either parent present. There were no complaints or other predicates for the raid. The fines, license revocations, and Stasi-style raids orchestrated by Governor Brown were pure retribution aimed at a citizen with the temerity to challenge her oppressive orders.

The pandemic- and lockdown-induced anxiety manifested in ways other than defiance, protests, and police action. On May 14, 2020, a Real-Clear Opinion Research poll was released that showed 40 percent of U.S. families were more likely to use homeschooling or distance learning when the pandemic subsided than to return to the public school system. As the lockdown extended to school closures in March 2020, parents had no choice but to use homeschooling or video learning to continue their children's educations. Neighborhood groups and co-ops formed to share the educational duties and take advantage of particular skills offered by some parents. These arrangements worked surprisingly well, to the point that many parents say they will continue homeschooling when the lockdown ends.

While parents and business owners were organizing against state edicts, states were organizing against their own citizens. Reuters reported that Arkansas, Hawaii, Kentucky, and West Virginia were considering the use of "GPS-enabled ankle bracelets or smartphone tracking apps" to impose house arrest on COVID-19 patients. An official of one of the technology providers suggested states sought to adapt house-arrest technology by "swapping out the word for 'arrestees' with 'patient,'" according to Reuters.

In early June 2020, a succession of retired senior military officers, including admirals and four-star generals, published bitter complaints and criticisms of the commander in chief. Prominent among these military critics was James N. Mattis, a retired four-star Marine general and former secretary of defense. He wrote, "Donald Trump is the first president in my lifetime who does not try to unite the American people. . . . Instead he tries to divide us. We are witnessing the consequences of three years without mature leadership." Eminent historian Victor Davis Hanson rebuked Mattis and other senior officers who made suggestions that were tantamount to treason (General James Clapper calling Trump a "Russian asset") or implied a coup d'état (Admiral William McRaven saying Trump should be removed from office "the sooner, the better"). Hanson cautioned, "In a time of crisis, their synchronized chorus of complaints, falsehoods, and partisan appeals to resistance threaten the very constitutional order they claim to revere."

Then the dam burst. On May 25, 2020, George Floyd, a forty-six-year-old African American, was killed in Minneapolis, Minnesota, at the hands of a white police officer, Derek Chauvin, during an arrest for allegedly passing counterfeit money. Three other officers assisted in the arrest and looked on as Chauvin pressed his knee on Floyd's neck for almost nine minutes while Floyd, who was handcuffed, begged for his life and said repeatedly, "I can't breathe." Within days the police officers were fired, Chauvin was charged with third-degree murder and manslaughter (with second-degree-murder charges added later), and the other officers were charged with aiding and abetting second-degree murder. Chauvin's bail was set at $1.25 million and the other officers' bail was set at $1 million each. The officers are awaiting trial.

The nation and the world erupted. The reaction was a mixture of peaceful protest, extremist violence, and criminal looting. Over 750 cities and towns across the United States and over 100 cities around the world saw protest demonstrations against racism and police brutality. Some turned violent as organized extremists (particularly a neofascist group called Antifa), and criminal gangs burned police cars, defaced landmarks, smashed store windows, and looted merchandise. By June 3, over 200 U.S. cities had imposed curfews. More than thirty states activated over 24,000 National Guard troops to quell unrest and riots. Over eleven thousand protesters and looters were arrested and more than twenty-one died as a direct result of the riots. On June 9, Antifa-led forces took over Seattle's city hall and established what they called the Capitol Hill Autonomous Zone (CHAZ) in the vicinity of the Seattle Police Department's East Precinct. The police fled the precinct house. Occupiers, some with weapons, set up a security perimeter using abandoned police barricades and improvised materials. Police withdrew from CHAZ and the homeless were invited. CHAZ quickly ran out of food.

From defiant hairstylists to armed occupiers of a major city, the anger, frustration, and insurgence of Americans has come pouring out in a mere ninety days. The history of racism in America is centuries old and was institutionalized and embedded in American culture long after the 1865 adoption of the Thirteenth Amendment to the Constitution, which ended slavery. Yet there have been many racial injustices that did not provoke either the breadth of peaceful protest or the depth of violence seen after the killing of George Floyd. It's too much to blame urban riots on COVID-19, just as it was too much to blame the Second World War on Woodrow Wilson's bout with the Spanish flu. Antifa was long waiting in the wings. Yet it's not too much to posit that fear of infection, the antisocial conditioning of quarantine and lockdown, and sheer uncertainty as to when or if the pandemic would end were contributing factors to nationwide social unrest on a scale not seen since the urban riots of 1968. Anxiety and depression are pervasive. If the Floyd killing was a match, lockdown fatigue was part of the kindling. Whether it's a Dallas stylist defying a judge or a bat-wielding extremist defying the NYPD, Americans are suffering psychosocial effects caused by politicians who seized on the pandemic to play petty dictator.

Unrest in the wake of the George Floyd killing would have been costly under any circumstances. The lives lost, smashed windows, looted goods, burned buildings, and devastated morale of business owners would be a heavy burden at the best of times. But these were not the best of times. Only a few businesses had tentatively reopened from the lockdown when Floyd was killed. Customers still lived in fear of the virus. To suffer ruin at the hands of rioters on the heels of a lockdown would be the last straw for many. A widely viewed video filmed from a car traversing midtown Manhattan showed block after block of high-end retailers boarded up like boardwalk bistros waiting for a hurricane to wash ashore. But the hurricane had come and gone, wearing a black helmet and with a crowbar in its hand. The damage was done. This social breakdown will prolong any recovery from the virus lockdown.

Wall Street Journal deputy editor Daniel Henninger perfectly captured the blended psychosocial impact of pandemic, depression, and social unrest in his column on July 22, 2020:

> There is a serious matter of civil order at issue here, but if you look beyond the mayhem, something else quite sad is happening. The irrepressible vitality of these cities—their reason for being—is

disappearing, undone by pandemic, lockdowns and a new culture
of permanent protest. . . .

Spike Wilmer, the owner-founder of two jewel-like jazz clubs in New
York's Greenwich Village, got the city exactly right:

> It's hard to describe but the feeling is gone, the vibe absent.
> The thing that made New York, New York is missing. . . .
>
> "It's very tense. People are very anxious and angry. Everything
> is closed or, if open, listless. There is no nightlife. If you leave your
> apartment after 9 p.m., it's a complete ghost town inhabited by
> wraiths and zombies, dangerous people."

The dangers of social disorder with attendant economic decay as a
consequence of the pandemic are global. London School of Economics
professor Branko Milanović described the socioeconomic linkage in *Foreign Affairs*:

> The economic repercussions of the novel coronavirus pan-
> demic must not be understood as an ordinary problem that mac-
> roeconomics can solve or alleviate. Rather, the world could be
> witnessing a fundamental shift in the very nature of the global
> economy. . . .
>
> . . . Lower interest rates can't make up the shortfall from work-
> ers who are not going to work—just as, if a factory were bombed
> in a war, a lower interest rate would not conjure up lost supply the
> following day, week or month.
>
> . . . The human toll of the disease will be the most important
> cost and the one that could lead to societal disintegration. Those
> who are left hopeless, jobless, and without assets could easily turn

against those who are better off. . . . If governments have to resort to using paramilitary or military forces to quell, for example, riots or attacks on property, societies could begin to disintegrate. . . .

. . . The most important role economic policy can play now is to keep social bonds strong under this extraordinary pressure.

Milanović's references to "military forces" and "riots or attacks on property" were written *before* the George Floyd riots. In hindsight, his words are chilling. Milanović is an economist with expertise in income distribution and inequality. His emphasis on the need to strengthen social bonds is identical to what clinicians and psychologists are advising with respect to the COVID-19 spread and the lockdown recovery. Economics and politics converged long ago. Now economics and medicine have joined hands.

In the conclusion to my 2019 book, *Aftermath*, I wrote:

It may be difficult to envision a worse scenario than 2008 and its aftermath, yet such scenarios are not infrequent—they have happened many times in U.S. history. . . .

. . . The scenario should include financial disruption, yet go beyond that as the consequences of greater scale in capital markets and faster contagion among networked institutions inevitably impact critical infrastructure and, finally, social order. . . .

Other catalysts include pandemic, war, and an out-of-the-blue failure of a major bank before the central bank ambulance can arrive at the scene. While each of those is a low probability event, the chance that none of them happens in the next several years is near zero. . . .

Sociologists and historians have documented civilization's thin veneer. Once critical systems break down, civilized behavior lasts three days. After that, the law of the jungle prevails. Citizens rely on violence, money, remoteness, or other forms of coercion to maintain their positions. . . . Our concern is not with the justice of this, but with the fact that in extreme circumstances it takes only days, not weeks, for armed quasi militias to flood the streets with violence. Civilization is barely skin deep.

In the final chapter we'll look at the question of where things will stand in the new economic order and provide specific direction on how to preserve wealth and how to prosper in the postpandemic world. This is not as difficult as it seems; rigorous analysis and early action are the keys.

Hugo Stinnes, a German industrialist, made a fortune during the worst stage of the Weimar hyperinflation in the early 1920s. He borrowed in reichsmarks and bought hard assets. The assets soared in value while the currency collapsed. He repaid the loans in worthless reichsmarks and kept the assets. His nickname in German was Inflationskönig, or "Inflation King."

In the late 1920s, Joseph P. Kennedy, father of President John F. Kennedy, made a fortune on Wall Street, first by ramping up stocks during the bubble, then by shorting them during the 1929 crash. Most investors were wiped out. Kennedy emerged richer than ever.

These cases show that money can be made even during hyperinflation and market crashes. The technique involves accurate forecasting, anticipating government's policy response, and nimbly investing ahead of the chaos. Investing is straightforward if you can foresee the policy response to a crisis. Seeing the policy response in advance is also plain if the forecast is accurate. Getting the forecast right is hard; that's where complexity models give investors an edge.

CHAPTER SIX

INVESTING IN A POST-PANDEMIC WORLD

The most extraordinary thing to my mind . . . was the dovetailing of the commonplace habits of our social order with the first beginnings of the series of events that was to topple that social order headlong.

—H. G. Wells, *The War of the Worlds* **(1898)**

W hile H. G. Wells's *The War of the Worlds* was written twenty years before the Spanish flu pandemic, it is routinely referred to in historical accounts of the flu. The reason is obvious. Wells described an invasion of Earth by Martians that was unstoppable. The Martians' spindly tripod war machines, complete with heat-ray devices and poison gas, were practically impervious to weaponry the military powers of the day could bring to bear. The Martians ran rampant, killing humans, destroying buildings, and burning farms. Then, just as humans were facing their own possible extinction, the Martians suddenly died. Wells describes the scene:

And, scattered about it, some in their overturned war-machines . . . were the Martians—*dead!*—slain by the putrefactive and disease bacteria against which their systems were unprepared; . . . slain, after all man's devices had failed, by the humblest things that God, in his wisdom, has put upon this earth.

. . . There are no bacteria in Mars, and directly these invaders arrived, directly they drank and fed, our microscopic allies began to work their overthrow. Already when I watched them they were irrevocably doomed.

Wells's work was extremely popular and well known worldwide. His phrase "disease bacteria against which their systems were unprepared" resonated with sufferers of the Spanish flu, which was believed by most scientists at the time to be caused by a bacterium; the virus theory was not proven until 1931, and no virus was seen by scientists until 1935, shortly after the invention of the electron microscope. Spanish-flu victims were as vulnerable as fictional Martians, and many suddenly died. Reference to *The War of the Worlds* is back in the news due to SARS-CoV-2, another lethal virus to which victims have no immunity.

Wells had another theme in his novel that was aimed at readers in 1898 and is highly relevant to investors today. This theme is the gap between perception and reality. It arises when one objective reality exists yet observers are either unprepared to accept reality or unaware of it. In *The War of the Worlds*, the Martians had indeed landed on Earth and begun assembling their war machines. Still, most humans either didn't believe it or didn't care. The news spread slowly in concentric circles from the Martian landing zone to local towns and finally to London and around the world. Still, the news was met with indifference or disbelief at every stage. Eventually reality sank in; by then it was too late. The Martians were on a rampage and there was no time to escape. Wells intended this as a warning—not about Martians but about technology and human indifference to the dangers it posed. The American social psychologist Leon Festinger gave this phenomenon the name "cognitive dissonance" in 1957, yet the phenomenon is as old as civilization.

Over time, the perception gap between reality and individual beliefs creates psychological tension. Either the observer must change his views to conform to reality or reality will overwhelm the observer, potentially causing great harm. It's like standing on railroad tracks and seeing a train approaching and somehow convincing yourself that's there no train, or it's not moving, or it will stop in time. In the end, the observer either decides it's a moving train and jumps off the tracks or is run over and killed.

THE PERCEPTION GAP IS THE KEY TO PROFITS

Cognitive dissonance is the best way to describe the behavior of most market participants today. On the one hand, the United States is experiencing its worst pandemic since the Spanish flu, the worst depression since the Great Depression, and the worst rioting since 1968 *at the same time*. On the other hand, major U.S. stock market indices recovered most of the February–March 2020 losses by early June; the NASDAQ Composite Index reached a new all-time high of 12,056 on September 2, 2020.

Stock market bulls claim the market is not looking at today; it's looking at the future and discounting that state of the world in today's prices. A positive forecast justifies the new bull market. That's the perception of some; the reality is entirely different.

Unemployment will decline, but it will decline from the highest levels in seventy-five years and not return to prepandemic levels for at least five years, perhaps longer. Growth will return but will be modest. The 2019 output level will not be reached until 2023 at the earliest. Lawyers are lining up at the bankruptcy courts to file a record number of large-business bankruptcy cases. Many small and medium-sized businesses will never reopen their doors, despite bailout money and soft loans. Price-to-earnings ratios for the S&P 500 stocks are at levels not seen since the early-2000 dot-com bubble. First-time retail investors are cashing IRS bailout checks and opening online brokerage accounts to buy Hertz, a company already in bankruptcy. New investor Dayanis Valdivieso said of her stimulus check, "It was basically free money, so, you know, I decided to play around with it. . . . It's like a gambling game." During bankruptcy proceedings, equity is often valued at zero. Yet novices like Valdivieso tripled their money as Hertz stock went from $0.72 per share to $5.50 per share on sheer speculation in the first week of June 2020. Hertz shares then collapsed when an NYSE delisting notice was issued on June 10. The novices got a quick education in bankruptcy and securities law.

As for the economy, which is it? A rapid recovery and return to normal with a great chance to buy stocks while they're still cheap? Or a slow recovery with weak growth, high unemployment, an output gap, and another stock bubble waiting to crash? Both scenarios can't be right. One must be reality and the other an exercise in denial. This gap between perception and reality is an example of cognitive dissonance as practiced by market participants. The perception gap creates huge opportunities for gains by investors. If the stock market has it right, the economy will soon boom and investors will see gains in commercial real estate, corporate credit, emerging markets, and the travel and hospitality industry. If the stock market has it wrong, the profitable opportunities will come from shorting stocks, buying Treasury notes, shorting the U.S. dollar, and buying gold. Which is it?

This thought experiment in cognitive dissonance demonstrates several essential facts for investors. The first is that you can make money in every kind of market. The idea that in bear markets you should quickly go to cash and move to the sidelines is untrue. That move will preserve wealth, yet an investor will miss out on profit-making opportunities that exist in bear markets. Unfortunately, investors are taught that stocks, notes, and cash are the only asset classes they can consider (and 401(k) plans are structured exactly that way). Yet there are liquid markets in property, private equity, alternative investments, natural resources, gold, currencies, fine art, royalties, insurance claims, and other asset classes. These asset classes don't just add range to tired allocations between stocks and bonds; they add true diversification, which is one of the few ways to increase returns without commensurately increasing risk.

The second lesson from cognitive dissonance is that profit opportunities are manifest if you understand that markets are not about being right or wrong; they're about information. There's a myth that markets are efficient venues for price discovery that smoothly process incoming information and adjust continuously to new price levels before investors can catch up and take advantage. That has never been true, and it's less true today than ever before. This "efficient markets hypothesis" was an idea dreamed up in the faculty lounge at the University of Chicago in the 1960s that has been propagated to generations of students ever since. It has no empirical support; it just seems elegant in closed-form equations. Markets are *not* efficient; they freeze up at the first sign of trouble. They do *not* move continuously between price levels; they gap up or down in huge percentage leaps. This can produce windfall profits for longs or wipeout losses for shorts. That's life; just don't pretend it's efficient. Most important, the efficient-markets hypothesis was used to herd investors into index funds, exchange-traded funds (ETFs), and passive investing based on the idea that "you can't beat the market" so you might as well just go along for the ride. That works for Wall Street wealth managers, who simply collect fees on account balances and new products. It does not work for investors who take 30 percent losses (or worse) every ten years or so and have to start over to rebuild lost wealth. You can beat the market using good forecasts, market timing, and a perfectly legal form of inside information. That's what pros do. That's what robots do. And everyday investors can do it too.

MARKETS ARE RARELY RIGHT

The fact is markets are more likely to be wrong than right in their forecasting. When markets get the forecast wrong, the gap between perception and reality can benefit investors. The 2007–9 financial crisis came into view in the spring of 2007 when mortgage delinquencies rose sharply. There was liquidity stress in August 2007; two mortgage hedge funds and a money market fund closed their doors around the same time. Then the problem seemed to go away. In September, Treasury secretary Hank Paulson announced the Super SIV (a roll-up special investment vehicle designed to refinance commercial bank off-balance-sheet liabilities; it never happened but sounded good at the time). Stocks hit a new all-time high in October 2007 (that's six months *after* the crisis started), partly based on unfounded assurances from Paulson and Ben Bernanke. In December 2007, a clutch of sovereign wealth funds from Abu Dhabi to Singapore bailed out the commercial banks by buying preferred stock and debt. All was well, or so it seemed.

Yet in March 2008, the investment bank Bear Stearns failed. It was quickly taken over by JPMorgan, and markets breathed a sigh of relief. Then in June, mortgage-finance giants Fannie Mae and Freddie Mac failed. Congress pushed through a bailout bill and markets again became complacent. Once more, the worst was over!

It was obvious we were witnessing sequential failures after the August 2007 warning. It was equally obvious that the failures were not over. Lehman Brothers had been the weakest link in the Wall Street chain since 1998 and was widely regarded by insiders as the next firm to fail in the new crisis. I explained this threat to John McCain's presidential campaign's economic team in August 2008. I was laughed off the call and not invited back. Markets continued to behave as if nothing were wrong.

Finally, on September 15, 2008, Lehman Brothers filed for bankruptcy. That was the point at which the gap between perception ("the crisis is over") and reality ("the crisis is just beginning") closed abruptly. Most investors got crushed. The point is that markets did *not* see it coming, and neither did Fed chair Bernanke, who said in 2007 that the mortgage problems would blow over. Markets were not efficient discounting mechanisms of future events. Cognitive dissonance had allowed investors to believe in the best outcomes while the truth was grim. Markets were in la-la land and got a brutal reality check that September.

Markets did not see the crash coming in 2008. And they did not see the crash coming in 2020. That's not what markets do. Understanding what's coming next is up to you.

HOW TO BEAT THE MARKET

How can you beat the market? There are three steps: Get the forecast right, get the policy reaction function right, and trade ahead of both. Those three steps are explained below using original models and optimal action plans. That technique is then turned into concrete investment recommendations.

Before diving into methodology and recommendations, one more piece of background advice is needed: *It is essential to stay informed and be nimble.*

The Wall Street mantra of "set it and forget it" is a great way to lose money. The idea that you can buy an index fund and "invest for the long term" is nonsense. When you lose 30 percent to 50 percent of your market value every ten years, there is no long term. Just because markets eventually regain their losses does not mean you should suffer losses in the first place. If the Dow Jones Industrial Average Index was at 29,000 and went down to 18,000, it might eventually get back to 29,000, but that could take five to ten years. Wall Street says, "Yeah, but you made your money back!" Not really. What happened is you ended up where you started after five years in Death Valley. What if you sold out at 28,000 (missing out on the rally's last 3.5 percent), bought back in at 19,000 (missing out on the first 5.5 percent of the new rally), and rode the market back to 29,000? Your incremental return during the market round-trip is 53 percent. The long-term investor who rode the market down and back up again made 0 percent. That's what Wall Street wealth managers never tell you. They just want your money in the account earning wrap fees. They don't care about you, your wealth, or your retirement.

This technique ("stay informed and stay nimble") is not limited to the stock market. It can be applied to every asset class, including bonds, private equity, and gold. I continually run into people who are surprised by a particular recommendation I make. They say, in effect, "Six months ago you said the opposite!" That's right. Ideas that were perfect six months ago may have performed as expected, producing significant profits, and now the time has come to close out the position, pocket profits, and try something new. This is particularly true in currency and commodity markets, where dollar prices can be range bound and subject to predictable reversals. The EUR/USD exchange rate may move between $1.00 and $1.60, but it will not go to zero like a bankrupt company or to exorbitant heights like Apple. Reversing course around critical pivot points is an essential trading technique. Markets change, conditions change, and news changes daily. You need to switch your portfolio mix in at least some respects to outperform markets.

This is not day-trading (which I do not endorse). The goal should not be to scalp nickels and dimes on a daily basis. Some traders are good at this, yet most lose their shirts. Instead it's a medium-term outlook (six months forward) with continual updating. This does not mean a position can't be profitable for five to ten years. It can. Nonetheless, you should be evaluating positions on a rolling six-month-forward basis to provide time to get out of the way of an oncoming train if needed. Markets don't do this well; they tend to get run over by the train and take investors down with them. Yet individual investors can execute this strategy with the right models and the right forward-looking trades.

A word on models: I have been extremely critical of most economic models for years. Models such as the Phillips curve, NAIRU, R-star, the "wealth effect," Black-Scholes, the "risk-free rate," and others are junk science. They bear no relationship to reality. They are a leading cause of the gap between perception and reality that leads to periodic shocks when reality breaks down the door of the faculty lounge. These models (which go under the name of dynamic stochastic general equilibrium, or DSGE, models) should be scrapped. They won't be, because three generations of academic economists have too much time and effort invested in their creation and perpetuation. That's okay; the academics' loss is your gain. If policy is guided by flawed models and you know the flaws, you can front-run the policy.

A word on diversification: It works. Diversification is a sure way to improve returns without adding commensurate risk. The problem is most investors don't understand what diversification is, and neither do their wealth managers. Your wealth manager will tell you that if you own thirty stocks spread among ten different sectors (say, energy, materials, industrials, consumer discretionary, etc.), you are diversified. You're not.

You may have thirty stocks spread among ten sectors, but they're all in equities, *which is one asset class.* Stock prices are increasingly correlated to one another and to the market as a whole. They rise and fall together. There are exceptions, yet not enough to mitigate the concentration risk. There are reasons for this correlated behavior, including passive investing, index investing, hot money, ETFs, and robots. You don't have to be expert on those causal factors. Just understand that buying different stocks does not give you diversification. True diversification comes not *within* an asset class but *across* asset classes. It's fine to have some stocks. Still, you should add bonds, gold, real estate, private equity, and other asset classes that are not highly correlated with stocks. That's how you improve returns.

A word on robots: Over 90 percent of all stock trading today is done not by humans but by robots. No matter how often the information is repeated, investors don't get it. These are not merely electronic order-matching systems that offer anonymity and cheap execution. Those have been around since the 1990s. Trading today is done by real robots that use coded algorithms to make buy and sell decisions and execute trades in nanoseconds without human intervention. When you make investment decisions, remember you're not competing with other investors; you're competing with robots.

That's good news because robots are dumb. They do exactly what they're told. When you hear the phrase "artificial intelligence," you should discount the word "intelligence" and focus on the word "artificial." Robots are programmed with code developed by engineers in Silicon Valley, many of whom have never set foot on Wall Street. They use large data sets, correlations, and regressions, and they read headlines and content for key words. When certain key words are encountered, or when price action deviates from a predetermined baseline, the robot is triggered and executes a buy or sell. That's about it.

Once you understand the robot algorithms, it's easy to front-run them. Robots assume the future resembles the past. It doesn't. Human nature may not change, yet conditions change all the time. That's why we have history. Robots assume that the people who utter the key words know what they're doing, but they don't. The Fed has the worst forecasting record of any major economic institution; the IMF is no better. Official forecasts should always be listened to and never relied upon. The officials in charge have no idea what they are doing. The robots' massive databases may have a huge volume of data, but they don't go back very far in time. Twenty or thirty years is not enough to form a good baseline. Ninety years is better. Two hundred years is better still. Robots routinely "buy the dips," chase momentum, and believe the Fed. When you know that robots are leading markets over a cliff, you can front-run the inevitable correction and profit from the robots' blind spots. Once again, you profit from the gap between reality and perception.

A word on insider trading: It's legal (most of the time). Insider trading involves using material, nonpublic information to trade ahead of big moves and beat the market. It's illegal only if you steal the information or receive it from someone who breached a trusted relationship, such as a lawyer, accountant, director, officer, or just someone who had a "hot tip" where you believe that person got the information improperly. If you obtain information legally by developing it yourself using better analysis, better models, or proprietary systems that you invented or receive as a subscriber, then you didn't steal the information and it's perfectly legal to trade on it. In fact, academic research shows that trading ahead of markets on inside information is the *only* way to beat the market. That results from a combination of good models and market timing. That's the key to outperformance. Yet it also explains why you need to be nimble, because model output is always changing based on updated information and conditional correlations.

To summarize:

Use models that work (as described below).

Update continually (with a rolling six-month horizon).

Diversify (across asset classes, not within one asset class).

Acquire proprietary inside information (legally).

Use market timing (to beat the crowd).

Front-run the robots (they're not that smart).

Own the perception gap (reality always wins in the end).

Be nimble.

That's the playbook. Now let's look at specific models and specific portfolio allocations.

A PREDICTIVE ANALYTIC MODEL

The prior section described the defective models used by policy makers and Wall Street wealth managers. So what forecasting models actually work?

Our model-construction technique uses four branches of science that are consistent with reality and can also solve for uncertainty. The first branch is complexity theory. This teaches that outcomes in complex dynamic systems are unpredictable as to timing yet are highly predictable as to the degree distribution of shocks. In plain English, this means that large market-moving events happen more frequently than normal distribution (the "bell curve") or equilibrium (DSGE) models predict. If the bell-curve model expects that an extreme event will happen once every hundred years, yet you know (using complexity theory and the power curve) that the event will happen once every seven to ten years, then you will be well positioned to profit from the event while others are running around yelling, "Black swan!" (a content-free cliché that even those yelling it can't explain). Complexity theory also teaches that the nature of extreme events (emergent properties) cannot be inferred from complete knowledge of the factors in the system. That's why shocks are not only more frequent than Wall Street expects but also different in kind. That doesn't mean you can predict the next shock with precision. It does mean you can expect the unexpected with some frequency. That alone makes you a better investor.

The second branch in model construction is Bayes' theorem, a formula from applied mathematics. Bayes' theorem is the tool you use when you don't have enough information to solve a problem by deduction. If all the information needed to solve a problem were right in front of you, a bright high-school student could solve it. What do you do when you don't have that much information (which is most of the time)? What do you do when you don't have *any* information? That's where Bayes' theorem is used. Bayes' also helps to overcome the uncertainty factor in complexity theory. That's why they work well together. I learned to use Bayes' while working in the U.S. intelligence community from 2003 to 2014. The CIA and the Los Alamos National Laboratory use it for everything, from counterterrorism to nuclear-explosion simulations, unlike Wall Street, which scarcely uses it at all. Again, Wall Street's loss is your gain.

You begin working the problem by making an intelligent guess about the answer, expressed as a probability based on experience, history, intuition, anecdote, or whatever data scraps you have. Conventional statisticians and academic economists disdain the guessing part; they demand more data. Yet when you don't have data and the problem is too important to leave on the shelf, a smart guess is the best you can do. Next you update the a priori guess with posterior information. When the new data arrives, you ask yourself: What is the conditional probability that the second data point would appear if the first guess were true (or false)? This is challenging because you have to be honest with yourself (if the original guess was wrong) and avoid confirmation bias (evaluate all new data, not just the bits you agree with). Humility is your best friend at this stage.

Eventually the likelihood of the guess being right goes down (in which case you discard it) or increases (in which case you can bet real money). When the likelihood of the guess being right reaches 90 percent, you can even go on TV and make categorical forecasts, as I did in 2016 when I correctly predicted Trump would win that election and that UK voters would vote for Brexit (both correct forecasts, which were made in the face of overwhelming odds favoring Hillary Clinton and "remain" in the UK vote). In both cases, I did not rely exclusively on polls but used anecdotal information, such as counting yard signs from a Greyhound bus, visiting an Evangelical compound in the Ozark Mountains, and holding everyday conversations with taxi drivers, hotel clerks, and London barmen. My advice to Wall Street analysts is to get out of the office more and get away from their screens. Few follow that advice.

The third branch is history. Academic economists and Wall Street analysts despise history or simply ignore it because it can't be quantified and used in equations. That's their loss; there's no better teacher than history. Individual story lines may not repeat, but the pattern does. History may be difficult to quantify, yet you can use it to create factor nodes in a cognitive map. The strength of the interactions of those nodes with other nodes *can* be quantified. Complexity theory can help one draw the map, and Bayes' theorem can be used to assign numeric strength to the nodal outputs. This illustrates how branches of science work together on an interdisciplinary basis.

It's interesting to hear analysts today refer to the Thucydides trap, an idea advanced by author Graham Allison. He uses the fifth-century B.C. Peloponnesian War between a rising power (Athens) and an established power (Sparta) as a warning of a coming conflict between a new rising power (China) and today's established power (the United States). That's a good example of how history can be used to enrich macroanalysis today. For forecasting purposes, I remind readers that Sparta won in part because of a pandemic.

The fourth branch is behavioral psychology. This is a field that has received enormous attention in economics and almost no application in macroeconomic models. In some ways, it's the scientific study of common sense, which reveals that people are often "irrational" as economists define the term. Well-designed experiments have been able to identify distinct cognitive biases and show that these biases guide human decision making, whether they make sense to economists or not. The most famous practitioners in the field today are Princeton professor (emeritus) and Nobel Prize winner Daniel Kahneman (who credits his deceased collaborator Amos Tversky) and Duke professor Dan Ariely. Among the many biases they identified are "confirmation bias" (we tend to accept data we agree with and discard data that we disagree with), "anchoring bias" (we get stuck on an old idea and won't change despite contrary evidence), and "recency bias" (we are unduly influenced by the latest idea). If you sense that some of these biases contradict each other, you're right. That's part of the overall irrationality. These biases apply to a wide range of behaviors, but they are particularly useful in analyzing capital markets. Behavioral psychology helps to explain market bubbles (confirmation bias lets investors ignore warning signs) and market crashes (a loss-aversion bias causes investors to value avoiding loss more than they value making money). The work is compelling and highly useful. Behavioral science gets lip service on Wall Street and is discussed at cocktail parties, yet it's not used in most models. Standard risk-management models still assume that the future resembles the past, bubbles don't exist, and crashes are "hundred-year storms" (they actually happen all the time). In contrast to Wall Street, improved techniques embed the insights of behavioral psychology in predictive analytic models.

The fusion of complexity + Bayes' + history + psychology in the new models is just a beginning. From there one can construct cognitive maps consisting of nodes (individual cells that represent critical factors or tradable results) and edges (lines connecting the nodes in a dense network). Separate maps are created for each market or asset class (interest rates, stock indices, currencies, commodities, etc.). These maps are constructed under the guidance of subject-matter experts who have the best grasp of relevant factors. The edges are given a direction (A —> B) and assigned a weight. Some edges are omnidirectional due to recursive functions (A <—> B). The nodes contain coded instructions based on a new branch of applied mathematics. Finally, the nodal processing is populated with both market data and plain-language reading ability from massive news feeds more sophisticated than mere headline readers. Edge weights and nodes are updated continually to reflect market and political conditions. The tradable output node is typically geared to a six-month horizon, which can be lengthened or shortened as needed.

This is our predictive analytic system. It's not for day traders. The new models can't tell you what will happen tomorrow. They can tell you what will happen in six months. That allows an investor to trade ahead of markets, which is the key to consistent risk-adjusted profits and excess returns. And it's the key to avoiding meltdowns.

WHAT ARE THE MODELS TELLING US?

Here's a summary of our predictive analytic views for the postpandemic world of 2021 and 2022:

Deflation (or strong disinflation) will prevail.

Stocks have not hit bottom.

Interest rates will fall further.

Bonds will continue to rally.

Gold will go significantly higher.

The COVID-19 recovery will be slow and weak.

Unemployment will remain near 10 percent.

Commercial real estate will fall further.

Residential real estate is an attractive opportunity.

The dollar will be strong in the short run, weaker by 2022.

Oil will surprise to the upside based on output reductions and sanctions.

Following are specific portfolio allocations based on these predictive analytics:

Stocks

Stocks have further to fall. The April–September 2020 rally in stocks had several factors supporting it, yet none is sustainable and all are far removed from the on-the-ground reality of the U.S. economy and individuals' preferences.

The first driver of the stock rally is the influence of robots. The algorithms are designed to buy stocks on Fed ease, buy stocks on positive pronouncements by public officials, buy stocks on momentum, and buy stocks on pullbacks. This software did not anticipate a decline from Dow 29,551 on February 12, 2020, to Dow 18,591 on March 23—a 37 percent drawdown in less than six weeks. Still, the robots knew that every drawdown in eleven years had been followed by a Fed-supported rally. Once the Fed cut interest rates to zero at an unscheduled meeting on March 15, the robots had their green light to buy the dip. Congressional agreement on the $2.3 trillion CARES Act stimulus bill, signed into law on March 27, also confirmed to the robots that practically unlimited fiscal stimulus would accompany monetary stimulus. Fundamental analysis and earnings projections were unneeded; the algorithms saw money printing and deficit spending (with more on the way) and lifted stocks off the bottom. From there, further monetary and fiscal stimulus, combined with a positive narrative about a V-shaped recovery and pure momentum, carried stocks most of the way to their recent all-time highs. The second driver for stocks is an overly optimistic belief that the U.S. economy will trace a simple V shape and bounce back quickly from the March 2020 collapse. It's certainly the case that the stock market itself has traced a V, as if anticipating the economic bounce-back scenario.

There are three problems with this sanguine view. First, there is no evidence that a V-shaped economic recovery is in the cards. Modest recoveries from extremely low levels hardly constitute a bounce-back; they are to be expected. Gains so far have been slight and powered mainly by never-before-seen deficit spending and zero interest rates. Those boosts will not be repeated; you can only go to zero once without raising rates again. Fed chair Powell declared on June 10, 2020, that markets should not expect rate hikes before 2022. Further fiscal deficits are politically if not legally dead beyond the current baseline and continuation of some ongoing programs, such as higher unemployment benefits. With those tools off the table, there will be no recovery without increased aggregate demand from consumers and businesses. Neither are inclined to spend at the moment. The second problem is that even advocates of the V-shaped recovery project a flattish right leg of the V. It's more a shallow bounce than a quick return to the former level of total output. Third, stocks are being boosted by pure speculation from retail investors, momentum chasing by hedge funds, and the dominance of index funds that have no choice but to buy the index.

The problem is these dynamics are at odds with reality. Fiscal stimulus does not work because of excessive debt. Monetary stimulus does not work because of falling velocity. The economy and corporate earnings will recover slowly if at all. A perception gap has opened up between stock market prices and economic reality. Since reality won't budge, stock prices must fall to converge with reality. This won't happen overnight; reality checks take time.

Of course, some individual sectors and companies will outperform in this new drawdown. It may be expected that defense stocks will benefit from higher military spending as international tensions rise in hot spots like the Taiwan Strait, the South China Sea, North Korea, Syria, Iran, and Venezuela. U.S. adversaries will take advantage of preoccupation with the pandemic both to test the U.S. and to distract attention from their own pandemic problems. The natural-resource sector (oil, water, agriculture, mining) will benefit from a global scramble for necessities and commodity inputs as supply chains are disrupted and alternatives are sought. The technology sector is clearly least affected by the pandemic, yet those stocks are so richly priced it's not clear how much upside remains. Yet sheer momentum could carry them higher.

As fourth-quarter 2020 data emerges, and as the reality of slow growth, rising bankruptcies, nonperforming loans, persistent high unemployment, and deflation are taken into account, stocks will fall back to earth and the perception/reality gap will close. The improved models project the Dow at 16,000 and the S&P 500 at 1,750 by late 2021, with some outperformance in the defense, natural resource, and technology sectors.

Gold

Why gold?

That's a question I'm asked frequently. I sympathize with the interlocutors. The fact that people don't understand gold today is not their fault. Economic elites, policy makers, academics, and central bankers have closed ranks around the idea that gold is taboo. It's taught in mining colleges, but don't dare teach it in economics departments. If you have a kind word for gold in a monetary context, you are labeled a "gold nut," a "Neanderthal," or worse. You are excluded from the conversation.

It wasn't always this way. I was a graduate student in international economics in 1974. Observers believe that the gold standard ended on August 15, 1971, when President Nixon suspended the redemption of dollars for gold by foreign trading partners. That's not exactly what happened.

Nixon's announcement was a big deal. Still, he intended the suspension to be *temporary*, and he said so in his announcement. The idea was to call a time-out on redemptions, hold a new international monetary conference similar to Bretton Woods, devalue the dollar against gold and other currencies, then return to the gold standard at new exchange rates. I confirmed this plan with two of Nixon's advisers who were with him at Camp David in 1971 when he made the announcement. In recent years, I spoke with Kenneth Dam, an executive branch lawyer and later deputy secretary of the treasury, and the late Paul Volcker, undersecretary of the treasury for monetary affairs in 1971 and later Fed chairman. They confirmed that the suspension of gold redemptions was meant to be temporary, and the goal was to return to gold at new prices.

Some of what Nixon wanted did happen; some did not. The international conference took place in Washington, DC, in December 1971 and led to the Smithsonian Agreement. As a result of that agreement, the dollar was devalued from $35 per ounce of gold to $38 per ounce (later devalued to $42.22 per ounce), and the dollar was also devalued against the major currencies of Germany, Japan, and the UK.

Yet the return to a true gold standard never materialized. This was a chaotic time in the history of international monetary policy. Germany and Japan moved to floating exchange rates under the misguided influence of Milton Friedman, who did not understand the role of exchange rates in international trade and direct foreign investment. France dug in her heels and insisted on a return to a true gold standard. Nixon got caught up in his 1972 reelection campaign, followed closely by the Watergate scandal, so he lost focus on gold. In the end, the devaluation was on the books but official gold convertibility never returned.

This international monetary wrangling took a few years to play out. It was not until 1974 that the IMF officially declared gold was not a monetary asset (although the IMF carried thousands of tonnes of gold on its books in the 1970s, and retains 2,814 tonnes today, the third-largest gold hoard in the world after those of the United States and Germany).

The result was that my graduate school class was the last to be taught gold as a monetary asset. If you studied economics after that, gold was consigned to the history books. No one taught it and no one learned it. It's no surprise most investors don't understand gold today.

Yet gold did not entirely exit the scene. In 1974 President Ford signed a law that reversed President Franklin Delano Roosevelt's Executive Order 6102. FDR had made gold ownership by American citizens illegal in 1933. Gold was contraband. In 1974 President Ford legalized gold again. For the first time in over forty years, Americans could legally own gold coins and bars. The official gold standard was dead, but a new private gold standard had begun.

Now, with gold trading freely, we saw the beginning of bull and bear markets; these don't happen on a gold standard because the price is fixed.

The two great bull markets were 1971–80 (gold up 2,200 percent) and 1999–2011 (gold up 760 percent). Between these bull markets were two bear markets (1981–98 and 2011–15). Yet the long-term trend is undeniable. Since 1971, gold is up over 5,000 percent despite two bear-market episodes. Investors worried about day-to-day volatility in gold prices and occasional drawdowns are likely to miss this powerful long-term dynamic.

The third great bull market began on December 16, 2015, when gold bottomed at $1,050 per ounce after the prior bear market. Since then, gold's dollar value has gained over 90 percent. That's significant, but still a modest gain compared with the 2,200 percent and 760 percent gains in the last two bull markets. This pattern suggests the biggest gains in gold prices are yet to come.

No time series of prices moves in a straight line. A huge initial rally in gold from December 16, 2015, to July 6, 2016, was powered by both fears of a Hillary Clinton victory in the 2016 presidential race and a brief fear trade after the Brexit vote, on June 23, 2016. After that, gold sold off sharply on profit taking and higher interest rates from the Fed. Gold rallied back to $1,303 per ounce on the Hillary fear trade, then crashed again once Trump won the election. Trump's victory signaled that stocks were the place to be; gold retreated to $1,125 per ounce in the aftermath of Trump's 2016 election.

Gold traded sideways from early 2017 to early 2019 on a risk on / risk off dynamic and the tempo of the trade war between Trump and China. On June 20, 2019, gold hit $1,365 per ounce—exactly where it had been on July 8, 2016, just after Brexit. There were peaks and valleys along the way. Still, for the long-term investor, gold had moved sideways for three years. Then the gold price took off like a Roman candle. Gold soared to $2,000 per ounce by August 18, 2020, producing a 45 percent gain in just over one year. This gain was powered by low interest rates, fears of inflation, and ongoing concern about stocks due to the impact of the pandemic on earnings.

Where does gold go from here?

The price of gold is driven by three principal factors. The first is safe-haven buying, the so-called fear factor. This is actuated by geopolitical developments, financial warfare, market collapse, and the new pandemic. The second factor is the level of real interest rates, itself a function of nominal rates and inflation. Gold has no yield and competes with cash equivalents for investor dollars. When real rates are higher, cash becomes more attractive. That's a headwind for the dollar price of gold. The third factor consists of fundamental supply and demand. Gold is no different from other commodities in this regard. If supply is abundant and demand is weak because of poor sentiment, that's a headwind for the dollar price of gold. At any point in time, these three factors can align or not. All three might push for a higher gold price, all three might push gold lower, or the vectors may be mixed, with one or two factors acting as headwinds while a third gives gold a boost.

The fear factor is volatile. In the early stages of the pandemic, fear was one factor driving gold prices higher. Declining new-infection rates in the United States and a rising stock market in April–September 2020 then tempered the fear to some extent. This pause will not last. The combination of a weak recovery, a pullback in the stock market, a second wave of SARS-CoV-2 infections, and confrontation with China in East Asia will put fear on the front burner and boost gold prices in the near term.

Real interest rates had been a persistent headwind for gold because of the Fed's double dose of monetary tightening from 2015 to 2018 in the form of rate hikes and money-supply reduction. That's over. Now the Fed has set rates at zero (and will keep them there indefinitely) and the money supply doubled in a matter of months (to $7 trillion from $3.5 trillion). The real-rate headwind has become a tailwind, since even modest inflation will produce negative real rates when nominal rates are zero.

The third factor, fundamental supply and demand, has been positive for gold. China, Russia, Iran, Turkey, and other nations have been buying hundreds of tonnes of gold without so far triggering a price impact that could cause disorderly markets. At the same time, global mining output has flatlined. Annual global gold mining output has been flat at about 3,100 tonnes since 2015. This de facto ceiling on gold production is attributable to the fact that many gold-mining projects in the major producing nations (China, Australia, Russia, the United States, and Canada) were shut during the gold-price collapse in 2013. Some of that capacity is now coming back online, yet the process is slow. It can take five to seven years to acquire needed capital, permits, and the drilling and milling equipment needed to reopen closed mine production and start new mines. In the meantime, capacity is static as strong demand persists. That's a recipe for higher prices.

What will drive gold out of its recent pandemic consolidation pattern and push it firmly over $2,000 per ounce and headed higher? There are three drivers.

The first is a loss of confidence in the U.S. dollar in response to massive money printing to bail out investors in the pandemic. If central banks need to use gold as a reference point to restore confidence, the price will have to be $10,000 per ounce or higher. A lower price would force central banks to reduce their money supplies to maintain parity, which is highly deflationary.

The second driver is a simple continuation of the gold bull market. Using the prior two bull markets as reference points, an average of those gains and durations would put gold at $14,000 per ounce by 2025. There is no necessary connection between the prior bull markets and the current one, but their history does offer a useful baseline for forecasting.

The third driver is panic buying in response to a new disaster. This could take the form of a second wave of infections from SARS-CoV-2, failure of a gold ETF or the Commodity Exchange to honor physical delivery requirements, or an unexpected geopolitical flare-up. The gold market is not priced for any of these outcomes right now. It won't take all three events to drive gold higher. Any one will suffice. None of the three can be ruled out. These events or others would push gold well past $2,000 per ounce, on the way to $3,000 per ounce and ultimately higher for the reasons described above.

Gold-mining stocks generally follow the gold price higher or lower with a lag and leverage. As gold moves higher in 2021, gold stocks will also rally. Yet that stock rally will generally run six months or more behind the bullion rally. This implies gold-mining stocks will be significantly higher by late 2021. This is typically frustrating for gold-mining stock investors, who watch the bullion price running away and don't understand why mining shares are not following. They will; it just takes time. Gold shares also act as leveraged bets on gold bullion. This is because of the mix of fixed costs and variable costs in the mining industry itself. It takes time to produce enough revenue to cover fixed costs, yet once that is done, incremental revenue drops to the bottom line, net of variable costs (which can be relatively low). The market applies a multiple to recurring revenue that is reflected in the stock price. It's not unusual to see gold-mining shares go up 300 percent or more as gold moves 100 percent (again, with a lag).

These gold share-price dynamics compared with bullion are well established and won't change. This does not mean that gold-mining shares are an automatic winner once gold prices move further. Stocks are idiosyncratic. Not all mining companies are created equal. The single largest factor in price appreciation (apart from the gold price itself) is management and engineering expertise. Some gold miners are extremely well managed by seasoned teams with strong financial controls. Others are fly-by-night speculations, some have incompetent management, some are frauds. The gold price will be strong. Not all management teams are. Only gold-mining companies run by highly professional and experienced teams will be winners in the coming gold price boom. Subject to that gating issue, smaller miners are a better value because they can attract a takeover premium, as large miners find it easier to acquire reserves from the junior miners rather than discover them independently.

Physical gold bullion will move from $2,000 per ounce past $2,500 per ounce by early 2021. From there, further gains to $14,000 per ounce by 2025 are likely. That will produce 700 percent gains over the next four years. Shares of well-run gold-mining firms are likely to produce 2,000 percent gains over the same time period, with a six-month lag to advances in the bullion price.

Real Estate

Unlike physical gold, which is an element (atomic number 79) the same in all times and places, no two real estate parcels are alike. This makes real estate valuation more art than science. The key valuation variables are usage (residential or commercial), location, quality of construction, date of construction, occupancy, rents, financing costs, and fundamental factors including economic conditions and the level of interest rates. This can make diverse real estate investments either attractive or unattractive at the same time, depending on the mix of factors. There is no one-size-fits-all solution to real estate investing. That said, and based on our economic forecast, the following appears to be true.

Commercial real estate in general has further to fall. This is both because of the challenging environment from the pandemic lockdown and new depression and due to factors unique to the industry, including bankruptcy of major retailers, store closures even by solvent retailers, pull-backs by bank lenders, a de facto rent strike by tenants, pervasive lease renegotiation by remaining tenants, and general deflationary trends.

In addition to these persistent factors, there are onetime factors that further cloud the picture. Damage from the 2020 riots will extend the reopening phase of lockdown relief as tenants conduct both cleanup and renovation operations. Looting and property damage to high-end retailers will add to insurance costs. Some retailers will not reopen; others will relocate to lower-density areas, leaving an overhang of high-end shopping district vacancies. On June 21, 2020, luxury retailer Valentino sued its landlord at 693 Fifth Avenue in New York to break a long-term lease on four stories of opulent retail space. Valentino's contention was that "social and economic landscapes have been radically altered in a way that has drastically . . . hindered Valentino's ability to conduct high-end retail business." The lawsuit is a reminder of how quickly perceptions of retailers and customers can change, and why commercial real estate will remain distressed.

Alongside these retail headwinds, many commercial and manufacturing companies, from warehouses to assembly-line operations, will relocate from troubled cities such as Minneapolis and New York to safer cities and counties. This will take time, and some buildings will remain partially vacant in the meantime.

Damage to the travel, hospitality, resort, and gaming industries was an obvious consequence of the pandemic and lockdown. This damage will not be undone quickly. Reopenings will be staggered, former capacities will be reduced due to social distancing and other precautions, and consumers will not surge back to these venues even when reopenings are complete, due to residual infection fears and reduced discretionary income.

Beyond this, there will be a new standard when it comes to commercial office space. Employers and employees were surprised at the success of work-from-home arrangements. Despite costs in terms of lost social interactions, the benefits in terms of reduced need for high-cost prime office locations in major cities was obvious. Extensive reductions in demand for corporate office space will result.

Finally there is the overhang of prepandemic problems. The most prominent of these is the near failure of WeWork, a major office space operator with prime locations in most major U.S. cities. Its properties are mostly leased, not owned, yet the leases were entered with leverage near the market top in 2017–19. Demand for WeWork facilities is down across the board, because of both the failures of small-business tenants and the new acceptability of work-from-home models. WeWork is the largest office tenant in New York City, with over 8.9 million square feet of leased office space concentrated in Penn Plaza, Chelsea, Gramercy Park, and the Wall Street area, among other high-priced locations. Other new construction projects were undertaken in anticipation of WeWork as the prime tenant, including the glitzy six-story Dock 72 tech center in the Brooklyn Navy Yard. These and other leases will now be put on hold or go into arrears while WeWork reorganizes. The result will be further downward pressure on rents and increases in vacancies at the worst possible time.

Some cities, including Seattle, Minneapolis, Chicago, and New York, will be particularly hard hit by this blend of factors. Other cities, including Phoenix-Scottsdale, Miami, and Washington, DC, will do relatively better because they present attractive go-to options and better economic fundamentals. As always, location counts.

Commercial real estate will rebound, but not soon. Whatever the long-term prospects are, there's no point in investing until the bottom is in sight. No one can call an exact bottom. Still, we have enough information to know the bottom won't be before late 2021 at the earliest. It will take time for rent renegotiations, relocations, bankruptcies, evictions, and the work-from-home revolution to emerge in the form of lower prices. This is a sector to keep an eye on and for which to keep some dry powder in terms of cash and leverage available for opportunities. Patience will be rewarded compared with jumping in too soon.

Residential real estate is another matter. The urban-to-suburban (or exurban) migration is just beginning in response to COVID-19 (made worse by high-density locations), degrees of freedom allowed by the work-from-home ethic, and a desire to escape urban unrest and increased crime as the defund-police movement gathers momentum. Rock-bottom interest rates on mortgages in desirable locations, combined with sky-high taxes in cities victimized by riots, make the decision to move easier. This trend is also propelled by demographics: The average millennial is turning thirty years old in 2021, even as the oldest millennials approach forty years of age. Investment opportunities in existing housing are limited. Still, investment opportunities available in new housing construction in attractive towns with low taxes and good schools away from urban hot zones will produce attractive returns. As with gold-mining shares, seasoned management of construction and development companies among those offering investment units is a key differentiator. Attractive destinations in Arizona, Texas, and Florida will be in demand. And investors should not overlook attractive locations in the Pacific Northwest, the Rocky Mountains, and the mountains and seashores of New England, especially the zero-personal-income-tax states such as Washington, Wyoming, Tennessee, and New Hampshire.

In summary, commercial real estate that has not hit bottom yet will present attractive investment opportunities on a selective basis in late 2021. Residential real estate is attractive today, subject to seasoned talent in the offering management companies and desirable locations away from older cities and toward low-tax, low-cost regions.

Cash

Cash is the most underrated asset class in the mix. This is a mistake by investors, because cash will be among the best-performing asset classes for the next two to three years.

The reason cash is disparaged is because it has a low yield. That's true; the yield is close to zero. Yet that truism misses several points. The nominal yield may be zero, yet the real yield can be quite high in a deflationary environment. If you have $100,000 in the bank with a zero yield, your nominal yield is zero. But if we experience 2 percent deflation during a one-year holding period, then the real yield is 2 percent. The cash amount is unchanged, yet the purchasing power of that cash has risen by 2 percent (the decline in prices), so the real yield is positive 2 percent. The math is counterintuitive $(0 - (-2) = 2)$, but it works. In a deflationary world, other asset classes are likely to be losing value, while cash can yield in the low single digits in real terms. That's a winning allocation.

Another underrated advantage of cash is optionality. When you make an investment, it may work or it may not, but either way there is a cost to exit if you want to reallocate your assets. At a minimum, you will pay brokerage commissions or cross the bid/offer spread or both. In the case of an illiquid investment such as private equity, real estate, or a hedge fund, you may not be able to exit at all for several years. In contrast, cash has no exit fee. If you have it, you can be the nimble investor who can respond on short notice to an investment opportunity others may have overlooked or not seen coming. Cash is your call option on every asset class in the world. Optionality has value that most investors don't understand. Still, it's real and adds to the value of your cash hoard.

Finally, cash reduces your overall portfolio volatility. The nominal value of cash is unchanged in all states of the world (although the real value can fluctuate, as explained above). A diversified portfolio contains volatile assets, including stocks, gold, and bonds. Cash reduces portfolio volatility compared with the volatility of those separate asset classes. Functionally, it's the opposite of leverage, which increases portfolio volatility. There's enough volatility in the world today. Cash smooths out portfolio returns and helps investors sleep at night.

In summary, cash is not a sterile asset. It has real yields in deflation, it offers holders the ability to be nimble, and it reduces portfolio volatility. That's an attractive trifecta.

U.S. Treasury Notes

U.S. Treasury notes come in a range of maturities, from two-year notes to thirty-year bonds with diverse maturities in between. In general, a longer maturity provides higher yields at the cost of greater volatility (called "duration") in response to changes in interest rates. Longer maturities also offer greater potential for capital gains if rates fall or capital losses if rates rise. Maturities of five to ten years are a sweet spot offering good liquidity, slightly higher yields, and significant capital-gains potential.

The criticism of Treasury bonds, which we've heard with increasing shrillness for the past ten years, is that rates are so low they have nowhere to go but up. The bears recite the fact that we are at the end of the greatest bond bull market in history and are on the brink of a new super-bear market. They advise you to dump bonds, go short, buy equities, and enjoy the ride.

At least, that's what they did until March 2020. In fact, bond bears, including famous names such as Bill Gross, Jeff Gundlach, and Dan Ivascyn, have proved to be completely wrong. Interest rates are near all-time lows, while capital gains on Treasury notes have been historically large. Some of the lesser-known bond bears have been carried off the field feet-first as their funds failed and investors fled.

What did the bond bears miss? They failed to grasp the critical distinction between nominal yields and real yields. It's true that nominal yields have hit progressively lower levels for almost forty years. We've seen one of the greatest bond bull markets in history. As yields approached zero, it seemed as if the party must end. Yet real yields are not low at all; in fact, they're quite high, which is one reason the stock market crashed in the fourth quarter of 2018 and again in the first quarter of 2020. A real yield is the nominal yield (the rate you see in the media) minus inflation. I borrowed money in 1980 at 13 percent. Was that a high interest rate? Not at all. Inflation at the time was 15 percent and taxes were 50 percent (my interest was tax deductible). So my real after-tax rate was *negative* 8.5 percent ($13(0.50)-15 = -8.5$). The bank was paying me 8.5 percent to take its money. That's a low rate. Today, with lower tax rates and lower inflation, the real after-tax rate is about −0.75, which is orders of magnitude higher than the −8.50 percent I paid in 1980.

That said, can rates go even lower than they are today? The answer is they can, and they will. Lower rates bring the concept of negative rates into play. The market yield to maturity on a ten-year Treasury note can go deeply negative, even if the Federal Reserve stops at the zero bound and does not adopt a negative policy rate for Fed funds. The reason is that secondary-market buyers of notes that have positive nominal yields can offer sellers a premium that is greater than the value of the strip of interest payments. This produces a negative yield to maturity because the buyer never recovers his full premium from the future interest. The buyer's premium is a capital gain for the seller. In other words, the bull market in bonds has far to run, as long as deflation is a threat and real yields are too high to stimulate a recovery. Both conditions prevail today. The bull market in bonds is not dead. Long may she run.

———

The forgoing overview of market conditions, rigorous modeling, and accurate forecasting and the survey of asset classes provide visibility on an optimal portfolio asset allocation that is robust to deflation, is robust to inflation, preserves wealth in a continuing crisis, and provides attractive risk-adjusted returns in both the fast- and slow-recovery scenarios. It appears as follows:

Cash	30 percent of investible assets
Gold	10 percent of investible assets
Residential real estate	20 percent of investible assets
Treasury notes	20 percent of investible assets
Equities	10 percent of investible assets
Alternatives	10 percent of investible assets

Some caveats are in order. To start, the cash allocation may be temporary. It's designed to offer optionality, yet the time may come in late 2022 when the investor will have greater visibility and wish to pivot to equities (if the recovery exceeds expectations), gold (if inflation emerges sooner than expected), or commercial real estate. Gold and Treasury notes come closest to the "buy and hold" category. Gains in gold will play out over five years, so there's no need to change the allocation based on short-term volatility. Likewise, Treasury notes are a classic asymmetric trade. Rates may go down (as I expect), yet they almost certainly will not go up (as the Fed has promised), so you will either make money or retain wealth; the chances of losing are low. The equity allocation should be weighted to natural resources, mining, commodities, energy, water, agriculture, and defense. These are the true countercyclicals that will do well in bear markets and will outperform in bull markets. Real estate and gold are the inflation hedges. Treasury notes and cash are the deflation hedges. This portfolio offers true diversification, preserves wealth, is robust to shocks, and offers material upside potential. In an age of pandemic, depression, riots, and global threats, that's as good as it gets.

CONCLUSION

Government cannot restore prosperity. Only entrepreneurs and risk-takers can. Americans must master their fears of the virus and dare to go back to work. . . . Interest rates are low. Gas is as cheap as it's been in years. Inflation remains moribund. People are tired of being housebound. They want to get back to work to make and spend money.

All that is missing is confidence.

—Victor Davis Hanson, Townhall (May 14, 2020)

The COVID-19 pandemic and the New Great Depression, which are densely entwined, are more than just another episode in a long-running series of panics and crashes. One can easily make a list, starting with the 1929 stock market crash and first Great Depression, running through the October 1987 flash crash, the 1994 Tequila Crisis, the 1998 Russia-LTCM crisis, the 2000 dot-com crash, and the 2008 global financial crisis. Along the way the world suffered through the 1957 Asian flu, the 1968 Hong Kong flu, and the 2009 swine flu. The jaded observer might say there's nothing new about market crashes or pandemics, what we're going through has been seen before, and it's not different. This too shall pass.

That's a mistake. This convergence of viral and economic crises is different and worse. The first and most obvious difference is these crises are concurrent; in fact, one caused the other, with help from the misguided lockdown. There was no pandemic during the Great Depression. There was no market crash during the Asian flu. Those crises came sequentially, not concurrently. Now we have both a pandemic and a depression and are verging on social disorder as well. This is not mere coincidence. Complex system turbulence has a way of catalyzing turbulence in other complex systems. We saw a contained version of this in March 2011 in Fukushima, Japan, when an earthquake caused a tsunami, which caused a nuclear reactor meltdown, which caused a stock market crash. Four complex systems crashed into one another in a cascade of failures. A similar phenomenon is happening now with the pandemic, depression, and social unrest, except the scale is larger and it is not contained. This difference in scope and scale is not merely cumulative; it is exponential.

World history has turning points. The difference between a true turning point and just another crisis is not the event itself but what comes after. The 1962 Cuban Missile Crisis was a turning point; the Cold War was never the same after that crisis, which prompted a multidecade era of arms-control treaties designed to contain the arms race. The 1987 flash crash was not a turning point; not much changed except the introduction of circuit breakers on the New York Stock Exchange. The 1973 oil embargo was a turning point; it marked the emergence of oil as a geopolitical weapon and the creation of Henry Kissinger's petrodollar standard, which has prevailed ever since. The 2008 financial crisis was not a turning point; it came and went. It was not long before Wall Street was back to business as usual, fleecing savers and inflating asset bubbles. The 2020 pandemic-and-depression is a turning point because our lives will never be the same. It will take years for the full implications to play out, yet we will not return to business as usual. Depressions truly are different.

There is both good and bad in this new turning point. The bad is all around us. America was deeply polarized before the twin crises; she is more so now. Issues such as using masks to prevent the spread of the virus should have been confined to scientific quarters, with clear information provided to the American public. Instead, wearing a mask became a progressive conceit because it signaled respect for "science" and government control, while not wearing a mask became a conservative conceit because it signaled rejection of the nanny state and the embrace of "freedom." This division carried over into the broader debate on the lockdown, the reopening, and the public-policy response of massive monetary and fiscal stimulus. Emerging disorder, from Seattle to Atlanta, is as much a symptom of the social disconnectedness that arose during the lockdown as it is a new cause for concern. There has been no shortage of irony. Those who favored open borders with Mexico suddenly applauded when the governor of Rhode Island ordered state police to detain drivers with New York license plates. Perhaps Rhode Island should build a wall. Of course, the virus didn't care.

The good news is that the situation is so grave and the challenge so daunting that this may be a time for Americans to work together for the good of America rather than the good of an ideology. There were many contributors to Allied victory in the Second World War, including brave troops, bold leaders, and the steadfastness of the UK when Britain and the Commonwealth stood almost alone. Yet historians concur that the single most salient factor was the U.S. industrial economy. The near-socialist FDR worked hand in glove with capitalist icons like Henry Ford,

Henry Kaiser, and others to produce ships, planes, tanks, bombs, and other weapons of war in such abundance that the United States and its allies simply overwhelmed the Germans, Italians, and Japanese. Our enemies couldn't keep up. During the war we were all Americans, down to young homemakers with small children who tended victory gardens in their backyards so large-scale agricultural providers would be free to feed the troops. There was time enough for politics after the war. This cooperative approach requires leaders on both sides to put acrimony and bitterness aside. There's no sign of this yet. Still, the crisis will linger and the needed comity may emerge in the fullness of time.

This book has explored viral science, reasons for the pandemic, the debacle of the lockdown, the depths of the depression, and the likely failure of monetary and fiscal policy in response. We have widened the aperture to consider the rise of social disorder and how this will extend the depression by destroying confidence just as businesspeople are emerging from their bunkers. Finally, this book has offered specific guidance on how to preserve wealth and prosper in the postpandemic world using an optimal blend of predictive analytic models, diversification, and common sense. All three are in short supply among wealth managers and bankers.

Before settling on a solution to the U.S. and global depression, one must first identify the specific source of the problem. America's greatest economic problem today is debt. The size of the debt blunts monetary and fiscal policy. Monetary policy fails because concern about debt causes Americans to save rather than spend. This kills velocity and makes money printing impotent. Low rates don't help, because that forces more precautionary saving to meet personal goals. Fiscal policy fails for the same reason. With debt levels so high, Americans expect default, higher taxes, or inflation. All three outcomes are reasons to save more today in anticipation of bad outcomes in the future. The U.S. economy is in a liquidity trap, and it's worse than the one that existed in the 1930s because the government can't replace the consumer; the government is the point at issue.

Repudiating U.S. debt is unnecessary because the United States can still print the dollars needed to pay it. Higher taxes could help defease debt, but taxes would kill the economy in other ways and do more harm than good. It is possible to grow your way out of debt (as the United States did from 1945 to 1980), but it takes inflation to do so. Debt is a nominal problem, and inflation provides nominal growth even if it does not provide real growth. Real growth can follow once the nominal debt is under control. If inflation can be created at a rate higher than interest rates (a condition called financial repression), the debt just melts away. A condition of, say, 4 percent inflation with 2 percent interest rates will cut the real burden of debt in half in thirty-five years. The Fed can take care of interest rates. It has no idea how to cause inflation.

To be clear, this is not about "paying off the national debt." That's completely unnecessary; the last time the United States was debt free was 1837. What is necessary is to make the national debt sustainable. The debt can grow in nominal terms as long as the real value of the debt is shrinking and the debt-to-GDP ratio is declining. Real growth can do this. Where real growth is not in reach, inflation and nominal growth work just fine.

So the problem is debt compounded by deflation. What is not clear is a way out of the wilderness, a solution to the new depression. Two presidents have found this solution—Franklin Delano Roosevelt and Richard Nixon—and the solution is there for the asking today. The solution is a dollar devaluation, not against another currency but against gold.

In 1933 the United States was facing a bank run and was at the end of the deepest deflationary episode in U.S. history. FDR became president in March 1933. He knew that Americans were hoarding gold to preserve wealth. As long as they were hoarding, they weren't spending—a condition similar to what we face today, except Americans now hoard dollars in bank accounts instead of gold bars. FDR issued an executive order demanding that all gold be sold to the U.S. Treasury at a fixed price of $20.67 per ounce, payable in paper money that could not be converted back to gold. In the same way the Fed today injects liquidity by buying bonds, FDR injected liquidity by buying gold. He didn't stop with the executive order. He continued buying gold on the open market. When gold became scarce in the United States, he bought more from foreign dealers. At every step, he acquired gold and injected dollars into the economy. FDR did something else. He gradually raised the price. As his gold purchases accelerated between October and December 1933, he moved the price up in small increments. Author Amity Shlaes tells this story in her book *The Forgotten Man*:

> One morning, FDR told his group he was thinking of raising the gold price by twenty-one cents. Why that figure? his entourage asked. "It's a lucky number," Roosevelt said, "because it's three times seven." As Morgenthau later wrote, "If anybody knew how we really set the gold price through a combination of lucky numbers, etc., I think they would be frightened."

What FDR understood, and his contemporaries did not, was that by raising the dollar price of gold, he was effectively *devaluing the dollar*. Economic shifts of that importance don't happen in isolation. If you devalue the dollar, the price of gold goes up, and *so does the price of everything else*. And that was FDR's goal. He needed to break the back of deflation by achieving inflation. The way to get inflation is to raise the dollar price of gold. The policy had very little to do with gold and everything to do with the dollar. On October 22, 1933, FDR conducted a radio

Fireside Chat in which he told Americans his plan was to "maintain continuous control of the dollar." Listeners took this to mean FDR's gold policy would continue. Wheat futures prices rose 40 percent before the broadcast was finished. FDR's policy worked. Prices rose, stocks rallied, and an economic recovery began (although recovery was derailed again by the Fed in 1938). Deflation was the enemy; inflation was FDR's friend, and FDR achieved inflation over the objection of banks and the Fed by raising the dollar price of gold. FDR ended his successful experiment in monetary policy in January 1934 with legislation that fixed the dollar price of gold at $35 per ounce, where it remained until 1971. The dollar price of gold rose 69.3 percent between March and December 1933. Measured by weight of gold, the dollar was devalued by 41 percent over the same period. A powerful inflationary wave had been created in just nine months.

Richard Nixon did the same starting in 1971, although the process was not completed until 1980, six years after he left office. Nixon faced different problems than FDR. Deflation was not a serious problem in 1971. Instead, there was a run on Fort Knox because foreign holders of U.S. dollars were losing confidence in the dollar-gold peg. Nixon closed the gold window on August 15, 1971, telling foreign holders of dollars they could invest in U.S. assets but "temporarily" could not have U.S. gold. Nixon's plan to devalue the dollar and establish a new gold peg, as FDR had done, fell apart. Trading partners transitioned to floating exchange rates, and the gold window never reopened. In 1974 Americans were allowed to own gold for the first time since 1933. It was the dawning of the age of a private gold standard rather than a government gold standard. FDR returned to a new gold standard after accomplishing his inflation goal, in effect putting the inflation genie back in the bottle. After 1971, the gold standard never returned. The inflation genie ran wild. Inflation hit 13.3 percent by 1979. Gold hit $800 per ounce in January 1980.

It took 18 percent interest rates and a severe recession in 1981–82 finally to get the inflation genie back in the bottle. It has not been seen since.

FDR's gold exercise was controlled and successful. Nixon's gold exercise was ad hoc and a massive failure. FDR stimulated growth and helped the United States find its way out of depression. Nixon created chaos, including borderline hyperinflation and three recessions from 1973 to 1981. This history shows that intervening in the dollar-gold relationship is like working the control rods on a nuclear reactor. If you do everything right, the reactor is a useful energy source. If you make one mistake, you can cause a meltdown.

It's nonsense to suggest that the dollar can be devalued against the euro or yen. If you weaken the dollar against the euro, that simply strengthens the euro and kills European economies with higher prices for their exports and tourism. The same is true with the yen. Retaliation by those trading partners is just a matter of time. Currency wars don't work. They are worse than a zero-sum game; they are a negative-sum game. The truth is that all paper currencies are in the same boat. They cannot all devalue against one another at the same time; that's a mathematical impossibility. If you want to devalue multiple currencies at the same time to cause inflation and reduce the debt burden, you need an objective measuring rod that's not one of those currencies and can't fight back. That measuring rod is gold.

Economists have spent three generations disparaging gold, so they have forgotten what a useful monetary tool it can be. The canard that you cannot have a gold standard and a discretionary monetary policy is false. The United States had both from 1913 to 1971. The claim that the gold standard either caused the Great Depression or limited the monetary policy response is also false. During the Great Depression, base money supply was allowed to be 250 percent of the U.S. gold hoard, valued at $20.67 per ounce. At no time did the money supply exceed 100 percent.

In other words, the Fed could have doubled the money supply at the time under the existing gold standard yet failed to do so. Don't blame gold for the Great Depression; blame the Fed.

Besides, an increase in the dollar price of gold today does not require a new gold standard. The Fed could simply buy gold at progressively higher prices after making its intentions known in advance. This is a straightforward open-market operation using gold instead of Treasury notes. As the gold price increased, the dollar would be devalued (as would other currencies) and inflation would arrive like clockwork. The inflation would melt the debt, the depression would end, and real growth would resume. Don't hold your breath waiting for this program. It's beyond the comprehension of U.S. central bankers (although Russian and Chinese central bankers are hard at work buying all the gold they can source). You don't need to wait for the central banks. You can buy gold yourself today. If the United States decides to raise the price of gold, you win. If the United States does not raise the price of gold, it will go up anyway because of debt and lost confidence in the dollar. Again, you win.

The pandemic will fade, perhaps not as quickly as some expect. A more lethal second wave is a possibility. Let's pray it doesn't happen. The depression will fade, but not anytime soon. Growth will be persistently weak; unemployment will be persistently high. Social life will resume, but it will not be the same. We'll get used to it, but it won't be the same. Social disorder will grow worse, at which point America will face hard choices about getting it under control. The one certainty is that the longer America waits, the harder those choices will be. The factor that will not fade freely is the debt burden. Debt leads to deflation, which worsens the burden. The answer is to use inflation to break the back of deflation. FDR showed us how to achieve that. His solution was gold. Our solution today is the same.

ACKNOWLEDGMENTS

This book was completed in far less time than my previous books, maybe less time than any book of comparable complexity in recent years. This does not mean I cut corners or sacrificed quality; I didn't. It does mean our team both inside and outside Portfolio worked together seamlessly, as if executing a two-minute drill from deep in our own territory while behind in the score. Thanks to that effort, the team scored.

I'm grateful for the support of the team at Portfolio/Penguin Random House, including publisher Adrian Zackheim, editorial director Niki Papadopoulos, and editorial assistant Kimberly Meilun. Their amazing efforts were complemented brilliantly by the help of my business manager and media adviser, Ali Rickards, and my editor, William Rickards. As always, the book would not have happened at all without the catalytic spark of my star agent, Melissa Flashman.

I'm fortunate to have a network of correspondents, social media connections, colleagues, and friends who keep me well supplied with analyses, news, and technical work I might otherwise have missed. When they know I'm working on a book, the flow of information becomes a flood, for which I am grateful. The group includes Art Santelli,

ACKNOWLEDGMENTS

Larry White, Chris Whalen, Dave "Davos" Nolan, TraderStef, Velina Tchakarova, Maryam Zadeh, Chris Blasi, Terry Rickard, Stephen "Sarge" Guilfoyle, Ronnie Stoeferle, and Mark Valek. Thank you all.

Writing in the time of COVID has its own challenges, beyond the usual need for a quiet place with a decent view to think and write. The lockdown made things too quiet and too isolated. Social interaction is crucial when you're describing the decline of social interaction. This is one reason why large families are a blessing. We may quarantine the world, but not one another. Writing is a marathon, and I could not have stayed the course without the love and support of my wife, Ann; my son Scott, his wife, Dominique, and their children, Thomas, Samuel, James, and Pippa; my daughter, Ali, and her husband, Rob (and their kittens, Pliny and Leo); and my son Will and his wife, Abby (and their pups, Ollie and Reese). They were all there for me, in person or in spirit, face-to-face or via video, and gave me the encouragement needed to cross the finish line. I love you all.

And if there are any mistakes in this book, they're on me.

NOTES

INTRODUCTION

xiii **Historically, pandemics have:** Arundhati Roy, "The Pandemic Is a Portal," *Financial Times*, April 3, 2020, www.ft.com/content/10d8f5e8-74eb-11ea-95fe -fcd274e920ca.

xiii **It is going to be hard:** "There Is Nothing Unprecedented About the Virus Itself," *Spiked*, May 11, 2020, www.spiked-online.com/2020/05/11/there-is-nothing -unprecedented-about-the-virus-itself/.

xv **the virus (SARS-CoV-2):** The technical name for the virus is SARS-CoV-2, while the technical name for the disease caused by the virus is COVID-19. The meanings of those terms and the distinction between naming a virus and naming a disease caused by a virus are explained in World Health Organization, "Naming the Coronavirus Disease (COVID-19) and the Virus That Causes It," no date, www.who.int/emergencies/diseases/novel-coronavirus-2019/technical -guidance/naming-the-coronavirus-disease-(covid-2019)-and-the-virus-that -causes-it.

xv **They know a lot *about* viruses:** See John M. Barry, *The Great Influenza: The Story of the Deadliest Pandemic in History* (New York: Penguin Books, 2018), chapter 7, for the extended discussion of the composition and behavior of viruses on which this description is based.

xv **Viruses do not eat:** Barry, *Great Influenza*, 98–99.

xix **John Maynard Keynes offered:** John Maynard Keynes, *The General Theory of Employment, Interest, and Money* (New York: Harvest/Harcourt, 1964), 249.

xxi **Known then as the Hong Kong flu:** See Sino Biological, "Hong Kong Flu (1968 Influenza Pandemic)," no date, www.sinobiological.com/research/virus/1968

-influenza-pandemic-hong-kong-flu; and Eric Spitznagel, "Why American Life Went On as Normal During the Killer Pandemic of 1969," *New York Post*, May 16, 2020, https://nypost.com/2020/05/16/why-life-went-on-as-normal-during -the-killer-pandemic-of-1969/.

CHAPTER ONE: A NEW VIRUS—FROM CHINA TO A TOWN NEAR YOU

1 **"All real scientists exist":** John M. Barry, *The Great Influenza: The Story of the Deadliest Pandemic in History*, (New York: Penguin Books, 2018), 262.

3 **"It was hard to believe":** Hannah Hagemann, "U.K. 's Boris Johnson Says His Battle with Coronavirus 'Could Have Gone Either Way,'" NPR, May 3, 2020, www.npr.org/sections/coronavirus-live-updates/2020/05/03/849770082/u-k-s -boris-johnson-says-his-battle-with-coronavirus-could-have-gone-either-way.

3 **The evidence is now strong:** Sharon Begley, "New Analysis Recommends Less Reliance on Ventilators to Treat Coronavirus Patients," STAT, April 21, 2020, www.statnews.com/2020/04/21/coronavirus-analysis-recommends-less -reliance-on-ventilators/; and Arjen M. Dondorp et al., "Respiratory Support in Novel Coronavirus Disease (COVID-19) Patients, with a Focus on Resource-Limited Settings," *American Journal of Tropical Medicine and Hygiene* 102, no. 6 (June 3, 2020): 1191–97, www.ajtmh.org/content/journals/10.4269/ajtmh.20 -0283.

3 **"The virus's strange effects":** Betsey McKay and Daniela Hernandez, "Coronavirus Hijacks the Body from Head to Toe, Perplexing Doctors," *Wall Street Journal*, May 7, 2020, www.wsj.com/articles/coronavirus-hijacks-the-body-from -head-to-toe-perplexing-doctors-11588864248.

6 **Since January 2020, the Wuhan Institute:** Bill Gertz, "Wuhan lab 'most likely' coronavirus source, U.S. government analysis finds," *The Washington Times*, April 28, 2020, www.washingtontimes.com/news/2020/apr/28/wuhan -laboratory-most-likely-coronavirus-source-us/.

6 **The first officially documented:** Josephine Ma, "Coronavirus: China's First Confirmed Covid-19 Case Traced Back to November 17," *South China Morning Post*, March 13, 2020, www.scmp.com/news/china/society/article/3074991 /coronavirus-chinas-first-confirmed-covid-19-case-traced-back.

6 **Total confirmed cases in China:** Unless otherwise noted, all data on daily confirmed cases and fatalities in this chapter is from "COVID-19 Dashboard by the Center for Systems Science and Engineering (CSSE) at Johns Hopkins University (JHU)," https://gisanddata.maps.arcgis.com/apps/opsdashboard/index .html#/bda7594740fd40299423467b48e9ecf6.

7 **A study by the American Enterprise Institute:** Derek Scissors, "Estimating the True Number of China's COVID-19 Cases," American Enterprise Institute, April 2020, www.aei.org/wp-content/uploads/2020/04/Estimating-the-True -Number-of-Chinas-COVID-19-Cases.pdf.

7 **That data suggests 7,000 dead:** Steve Watson, "US Intel Officials Believe 45,000 Corpses Were Incinerated in One Fortnight in Wuhan," Summit News, April 28, 2020, https://summit.news/2020/04/28/us-intel-officials-believe-45500 -corpses-were-incinerated-in-one-fortnight-in-wuhan/.

7 **There have been eight:** See Kristine A. Moore et al., "The Future of the COVID-19 Pandemic: Lessons Learned from Pandemic Influenza," Center for Infectious Disease Research and Policy, University of Minnesota, April 30, 2020, www.cidrap.umn.edu/sites/default/files/public/downloads/cidrap-covid19 -viewpoint-part1_0.pdf.

9 **This expanded incubation period:** Moore et al., "Future of the COVID-19 Pandemic," 3.

10 **The R0 for the SARS-CoV-2 virus:** Roy M. Anderson et al., "How Will Country-Based Mitigation Measures Influence the Course of the COVID-19 Epidemic?" *The Lancet* 395, no. 10228 (March 21–27, 2020): 395.

11 **Based on the pattern:** See Moore et al., "Future of the COVID-19 Pandemic," 6.

13 **There is strong statistical:** See Marina Medvin, "Israeli Professor Shows Virus Follows Fixed Pattern," Townhall, April 15, 2020, https://townhall.com/colum nists/marinamedvin/2020/04/15/israeli-professor-shows-virus-follows-fixed -pattern-n2566915; and Isaac Ben-Israel, "The End of Exponential Growth: The Decline in the Spread of Coronavirus," *Times of Israel*, April 19, 2020, www. timesofisrael.com/the-end-of-exponential-growth-the-decline-in-the -spread-of-coronavirus/.

13 **"It's almost this":** Sheri Fink, "Hospitals Move into Next Phase as New York Passes Viral Peak," *New York Times*, May 20, 2020, www.nytimes.com/2020 /05/20/nyregion/hospitals-coronavirus-cases-decline.html.

13 **A scientific study released:** Lizhou Zhang et al., "The DG614G Mutation in the SARS-CoV-2 Spike Protein Reduces SI Shedding and Increases Infectivity," bioRxiv (preprint, not peer reviewed), June 12, 2020, www.biorxiv.org/content /10.1101/2020.06.12.148726v1.full.

14 **This mutation, known as the G variant:** Sarah Kaplan and Joel Achenbach, "This Coronavirus Mutation Has Taken Over the World. Scientists Are Trying to Understand Why," *Washington Post*, June 29, 2020, www.washingtonpost.com /science/2020/06/29/coronavirus-mutation-science/.

16 **When they did react:** For a comprehensive official overview of Chinese efforts to suppress information about the COVID-19 outbreak, destroy evidence of its possible source, punish and intimidate those who attempted to report accurately on the spread of the SARS-CoV-2 virus, and refuse cooperation with outside experts see, "The Origins of the COVID-19 Global Pandemic, Including the Roles of the Chinese Communist Party and the World Health Organization," House Foreign Affairs Committee Minority Staff Interim Report, June 12, 2020, www.hsdl.org/?view&did=840477.

16 **Instead of commending Li:** Stephanie Hegarty, "The Chinese Doctor Who

Tried to Warn Others About Coronavirus," BBC News, February 6, 2020, www .bbc.com/news/world-asia-china-51364382.

17 **Scientists estimate that 95 percent:** William Davis, "How China's Coronavirus Cover-Up Happened," Daily Caller, April 19, 2020, https://dailycaller.com /2020/04/19/coronavirus-china-activities-timeline-trump-cover-up/.

17 **"Preliminary investigations conducted":** Kieran Corcoran, "An Infamous WHO Tweet Saying There Was 'No Clear Evidence' COVID-19 Could Spread Between Humans Was Posted for 'Balance' to Reflect Findings from China," Business Insider, April 18, 2020, www.businessinsider.com/who-no-transmission -coronavirus-tweet-was-to-appease-china-guardian-2020-4.

17 **On January 30, 2020, WHO called:** Rachael Rettner, "Coronavirus Outbreak Is 'Public Health Emergency of International Concern,' WHO Declares," Live Science, January 30, 2020, www.livescience.com/who-coronavirus-outbreak -emergency-international-concern.html.

18 **"World Health Organization's role":** "Coronavirus: US to Halt Funding to WHO, Says Trump," BBC News, April 15, 2020, www.bbc.com/news/world-us -canada-52289056.

18 **"Chinese officials ignored":** Tom Howell and Dave Boyer, "Trump Pulls U.S. Out of World Health Organization, Slaps Penalties on China over Hong Kong Action," *Washington Times*, May 29, 2020, www.washingtontimes.com/news /2020/may/29/trump-pulls-us-out-world-health-organization-slaps/.

19 **Wet markets have been identified:** Robert G. Webster, "Wet Markets—a Continuing Source of Severe Acute Respiratory Syndrome and Influenza?" *The Lancet* 363, no. 9404 (January 17, 2004): 234–36, www.ncbi.nlm.nih.gov/pmc/articles /PMC7112390/.

20 **Risky experiments involving genetic engineering:** Shi Zehngli-Li et al., "A SARS-like Cluster of Circulating Bat Coronaviruses Shows Potential for Human Emergence," *Nature Medicine* 21, no. 12 (November 9, 2015): 1508–13, www.ncbi.nlm.nih.gov/pmc/articles/PMC4797993/.

20 **Dr. Shi's work has been:** Declan Butler, "Engineered Bat Virus Stirs Debate over Risky Research," *Nature*, November 12, 2015, www.nature.com/news /engineered-bat-virus-stirs-debate-over-risky-research-1.18787.

20 **"has a serious shortage":** Josh Rogin, "State Department Cables Warned of Safety Issues at Wuhan Lab Studying Bat Coronaviruses," *Washington Post*, April 14, 2020, www.washingtonpost.com/opinions/2020/04/14/state-department-cables -warned-safety-issues-wuhan-lab-studying-bat-coronaviruses/.

21 **"isolated and obtained some coronaviruses":** Lee Brown, "Wuhan Lab Admits to Having Three Live Strains of Bat Coronavirus on Site," *New York Post*, May 24, 2020, https://nypost.com/2020/05/24/wuhan-lab-admits-to-having -three-live-strains-of-bat-coronavirus/.

21 *Washington Post* **columnist David Ignatius:** David Ignatius, "How Did Covid-19

Begin? Its Initial Origin Story Is Shaky," *Washington Post*, April 2, 2020, www
.washingtonpost.com/opinions/global-opinions/how-did-covid-19-begin-its
-initial-origin-story-is-shaky/2020/04/02/1475d488-7521-11ea-87da
-77a8136c1a6d_story.html.

21 **The type of bat that carries:** Tom Cotton, "Coronavirus and the Laboratories
in Wuhan," *Wall Street Journal*, April 21, 2020, www.wsj.com/articles/corona
virus-and-the-laboratories-in-wuhan-11587486996.

21 *The Lancet* **published an article:** Chaolin Huang et al., "Clinical Features of
Patients Infected with 2019 Novel Coronavirus in Wuhan, China," *The Lancet*
395, no. 10223 (January 24, 2020): 497–506, www.thelancet.com/journals/lancet
/article/PIIS0140-6736(20)30183-5/fulltext#fig1.

21 **Gao Fu, the director:** Gu Liping, "Official: Wuhan Seafood Market May Be the
Victim of Coronavirus," Ecns.com, May 26, 2020, http://www.ecns.cn/news
/politics/2020-05-26/detail-ifzwqsxz6424882.shtml.

22 **One article claims to show:** Kristian G. Andersen et al., "The Proximal Origin
of SARS-CoV-2," *Nature Medicine* 26 (April 2020): 450, www.nature.com
/articles/s41591-020-0820-9.pdf.

22 **The study was partially funded:** Bill Gertz, "Coronavirus Origins in Lab Not
Ruled Out by Scientific Studies," *Washington Times*, April 21, 2020, www
.washingtontimes.com/news/2020/apr/20/coronavirus-origins-lab-not-ruled
-out-scientific-s/.

22 **A more recent study:** Sharri Markson, "Coronavirus May Have Been a 'Cell-
Culture Experiment' Gone Wrong," Sky News, May 24, 2020, www.skynews
.com.au/details/_6158843835001.

23 **"inserted sections placed":** B. Sørensen, A. Susrud, and A. G. Dalgleish,
"Biovacc-19: A Candidate Vaccine for Covid-19 (SARS-CoV-2) Developed
from Analysis of Its General Method of Action for Infectivity," *Quarterly
Review of Biophysics*, May 28, 2020, www.cambridge.org/core/services/aop
-cambridge-core/content/view/DBBC0FA6E3763B0067CAAD8F3363E527
/S2633289220000083a.pdf/biovacc19_a_candidate_vaccine_for_covid19
_sarscov2_developed_from_analysis_of_its_general_method_of_action_for
_infectivity.pdf.

23 **"the virus has properties":** David Nikel, "Controversial Coronavirus Lab Origin Claims Dismissed by Experts," *Forbes*, June 7, 2020, www.forbes.com/sites
/davidnikel/2020/06/07/norway-scientist-claims-report-proves-coronavirus
-was-lab-made/#7769e43c121d.

24 **Detailed scientific evidence:** Li-Meng Yan et. al., "Unusual Features of the
SARS-CoV-2 Genome Suggesting Sophisticated Laboratory Modification Rather
Than Natural Evolution and Delineation of Its Probable Synthetic Route," Rule
of Law Society & Rule of Law Foundation, *Zenodo*, September 14, 2020, https
://zenodo.org/record/4028830#.X21UKi2ZN-j. The ease with which lethal ge-

netic modification of the type suggested by Dr. Yan can be carried out is described in chilling detail in Richard Preston, *The Demon in the Freezer* (New York: Random House, 2002).

24 **"The Chinese government deliberately covered up"**: Sharri Markson, "Coronavirus NSW: Dossier Lays Out Case Against China Bat Virus Program," *Daily Telegraph*, May 3, 2020, www.dailytelegraph.com.au/coronavirus/bombshell-dossier-lays-out-case-against-chinese-bat-virus-program/news-story/55add857058731c9c71c0e96ad17da60.

24 **In mid-January 2020, near the height:** Minnie Chan and William Zheng, "Meet the Major General on China's Coronavirus Scientific Front Line," *South China Morning Post*, March 3, 2020, www.scmp.com/news/china/military/article/3064677/meet-major-general-chinas-coronavirus-scientific-front-line?mod=article_inline.

24 **China's propaganda plan:** Fu Ying, "Shape Global Narratives for Telling China's Stories," *China Daily*, April 4, 2020, https://global.chinadaily.com.cn/a/202004/21/WS5e9e313ba3105d50a3d178ab.html.

CHAPTER TWO: ONE HUNDRED DAYS—CHRONICLE OF A LOCKDOWN

27 **"Worldwide, the Spanish flu"**: Walter Scheidel, "The Spanish Flu Didn't Wreck the Global Economy," *Foreign Affairs*, May 28, 2020, https://www.foreignaffairs.com/articles/united-states/2020-05-28/spanish-flu-didnt-wreck-global-economy.

28 **Trump banned travel:** See Centers for Disease Control and Prevention, "Travelers Prohibited from Entry to the United States," updated June 15, 2020, www.cdc.gov/coronavirus/2019-ncov/travelers/from-other-countries.html.

29 **Michigan governor Gretchen Whitmer:** Michael J. Reitz, "What's Wrong with Gov. Whitmer's Stay-at-Home Order," Mackinac Center for Public Policy, April 15, 2020, www.mackinac.org/whats-wrong-with-gov-whitmers-stay-at-home-order.

29 **"NHs must comply"**: New York State Department of Health, "Advisory: Hospital Discharges and Admissions to Nursing Homes," March 25, 2020, http://www.hurlbutcare.com/images/NYSDOH_Notice.pdf.

29 **"No resident shall be denied"**: New York State Department of Health, "Advisory: Hospital Discharges and Admissions to ACFs," April 7, 2020, https://coronavirus.health.ny.gov/system/files/documents/2020/04/doh_covid19_acfreturnofpositiveresidents_040720.pdf.

30 **"was the single dumbest"**: Bernard Condon, Jennifer Peltz, and Jim Mustian, "AP count: Over 4,500 Virus Patients Sent to NY Nursing Homes," ABC News, May 22, 2020, https://abcnews.go.com/Health/wireStory/ap-count-4300-virus-patients-ny-nursing-homes-70825470.

31 **"No medicine and none"**: John M. Barry, *The Great Influenza: The Story of the Deadliest Pandemic in History* (New York: Penguin Books, 2018), 358–59.

33 **"I think the whole notion"**: Helen Branswell, "Why 'Flattening the Curve' May Be the World's Best Bet to Slow the Coronavirus," Stat, March 11, 2020, www.statnews.com/2020/03/11/flattening-curve-coronavirus/.

33 **"But, as horrific as the disease"**: Barry, *Great Influenza*, 460–61.

34 **"There aren't any vaccines"**: Hoover Institution, "Dr. Jay Bhattacharya: His New MLB COVID-19 Study and the Dilemma of the Lockdown," Uncommon Knowledge with Peter Robinson, May 11, 2020, www.youtube.com/watch?v=289NWm85eas&feature=youtu.be.

35 **A cure may be available:** Jo Kahn, "We've Never Made a Successful Vaccine for a Coronavirus Before. This Is Why It's so Difficult," ABC News, April 16, 2020, www.abc.net.au/news/health/2020-04-17/coronavirus-vaccine-ian-frazer /12146616.

35 **Two recent studies:** Quan-Xin Long et al., "Clinical and immunological assessment of asymptomatic SARS-CoV-2 infections," *Nature Medicine*, June 18, 2020, https://doi.org/10.1038/s41591-020-0965-6, and Marina Pollán et al., "Prevalence of SARS-CoV-2 in Spain (ENE-COVID): A Nationwide, Population-Based Seroepidemiological Study," July 6, 2020, www.thelancet.com/journals /lancet/article/PIIS0140-6736(20)31483-5/fulltext.

35 **A contributor to the Spanish study:** Adam Payne, "Coronavirus Herd Immunity May Be 'Unachievable' After Study Suggests Antibodies Disappear After Weeks in Some People," *Business Insider*, July 7, 2020, www.businessinsider.com /coronavirus-antibodies-study-herd-immunity-unachievable-spain-2020-7.

36 **That puts the overall:** See Centers for Disease Control and Prevention, "COVID-19 Pandemic Planning Scenarios," updated July 10, 2020, www.cdc.gov /coronavirus/2019-ncov/hcp/planning-scenarios.html.

36 **Another study published by *The Lancet***: Rabail Chaudhry et al., "A country level analysis measuring the impact of government actions, country preparedness and socioeconomic factors on COVID-19 mortality and related health outcomes," *EClinicalMedicine* published by *The Lancet*, July 21, 2020, https://www.thelancet .com/journals/eclinm/article/PIIS2589-5370(20)30208-X/fulltext.

37 **Findings presented by the American:** Audrey Redford and Thomas K. Duncan, "Drugs, Suicide and Crime: Empirical Estimates of the Human Toll of the Shutdown," American Institute for Economic Research, March 28, 2020, www .aier.org/article/drugs-suicide-and-crime-empirical-estimates-of-the-human -toll-of-the-shut-down/.

37 **"The numbers are unprecedented"**: Andrew Mark Miller, "California Doctors Say They've seen More Deaths from Suicide Than Coronavirus Since Lockdowns," *Washington Examiner*, May 21, 2020, www.washingtonexaminer.com/ news/california-doctors-say-theyve-seen-more-deaths-from-suicide-than -coronavirus-since-lockdowns.

38 **"Masks are not 100 percent"**: Alexandra Kelley, "Fauci: Why the Public Wasn't Told to Wear Masks When the Coronavirus Pandemic Began," The Hill,

June 16, 2020, https://thehill.com/changing-america/well-being/prevention-cures/502890-fauci-why-the-public-wasnt-told-to-wear-masks.

38 **"You don't need a mask":** Lisa Lerer, "'It's a Pandemic, Stupid,'" *New York Times*, June 25, 2020, www.nytimes.com/2020/06/25/us/politics/tom-frieden-coronavirus.html.

38 **"Trump and his party":** Paul Krugman, "How Many Will Die for the Dow?" *New York Times*, May 21, 2020, www.nytimes.com/2020/05/21/opinion/trump-coronavirus-dow.html.

39 **The CDC previewed a plan:** Robert J. Glass et al., "Targeted Social Distancing Designs for Pandemic Influenza," *Emerging Infectious Diseases* 12, no. 11 (November 2006): 1671–81, https://www.cdc.gov/eid/article/12/11/06-0255_article.

39 **"error of judgement":** "Coronavirus: Prof. Neil Ferguson Quits Government Role After 'Undermining' Lockdown," BBC News, May 6, 2020, www.bbc.com/news/uk-politics-52553229.

39 **The CDC paper then became:** Centers for Disease Control and Prevention, "Interim Pre-pandemic Planning Guidance: Community Strategy for Pandemic Influenza Mitigation in the United States—Early, Targeted, Layered Use of Non-pharmaceutical Interventions," February 2007, www.cdc.gov/flu/pandemic-resources/pdf/community_mitigation-sm.pdf.

39 **Bush had read a detailed history:** Eric Lipton and Jennifer Steinhauer, "The Untold Story of the Birth of Social Distancing," *New York Times*, April 22, 2020 www.nytimes.com/2020/04/22/us/politics/social-distancing-coronavirus.html.

39 **The Bush plan was updated:** Noreen Qualls et al., "Community Mitigation Guidelines to Prevent Pandemic Influenza—United States, 2017," *Morbidity and Mortality Weekly Report* 66, no. 1 (April 21, 2017): 1–34, www.cdc.gov/mmwr/volumes/66/rr/rr6601a1.htm.

40 **The 2017 final plan's:** Centers for Disease Control and Prevention, "Frequently Asked Questions: Pandemic Flu and the Updated Community Mitigation Guidelines," August 3, 2017, www.cdc.gov/nonpharmaceutical-interventions/tools-resources/faq-pandemic-flu.html.

40 **Henderson coauthored a paper:** Thomas V. Inglesby et al., "Disease Mitigation Measures in the Control of Pandemic Influenza," *Biosecurity and Bioterrorism: Biodefense Strategy, Practice, and Science* 4, no. 4 (2006), https://pubmed.ncbi.nlm.nih.gov/17238820/.

41 **"In a future flu pandemic":** Laura Spinney, *Pale Rider: The Spanish Flu of 1918 and How It Changed the World* (New York: Public Affairs, 2017): 281–84.

CHAPTER THREE: THE NEW GREAT DEPRESSION

45 **"Only a few months into":** Mohamed A. El-Erian, "Wall Street Is Flourishing While Main Street Is Suffering," *Foreign Policy*, May 29, 2020, https://foreignpolicy.com/2020/05/29/stock-market-rally-coronavirus-pandemic/.

55 **On September 21, 2020:** Bernadette Hogan, "Almost 90 Percent of NYC Bars and Restaurants Couldn't Pay August Rent," *New York Post*, September 21, 2020, https://nypost.com/2020/09/21/almost-90-percent-of-nyc-bars-and-res taurants-couldnt-pay-august-rent/.

55 **Already this depression has claimed:** Hannah Miller and Christina Cheddar Berk, "JC Penney Could Join a Growing List of Bankruptcies During the Coro- navirus Pandemic," CNBC, May 15, 2020, www.cnbc.com/2020/05/15/these -companies-have-filed-for-bankruptcy-since-the-coronavirus-pandemic.html.

56 **On June 8, 2020, the National:** "Determination of the February 2020 Peak in U.S. Economic Activity," *National Bureau of Economic Research*, June 8, 2020, www.nber.org/cycles/june2020.html.

56 **The highly regarded economic research firm:** "Sharpest Monthly Contraction in World Trade on Record," *Capital Economics*, June 25, 2020, www.capitaleco nomics.com/clients/publications/global-economics/global-trade-monitor /sharpest-monthly-contraction-in-world-trade-on-record/.

58 **On June 24, 2020, the IMF:** Martin Crutsinger, "IMF Downgrades Outlook for Global Economy in Face of Virus," Associated Press, June 24, 2020, https:// apnews.com/2be55cbdf80ca8049655570c6f756027.

58 **On June 24, 2020, New York City:** Dana Rubinstein and Christina Goldbaum, "Pandemic May Force New York City to Lay Off 22,000 Workers," *New York Times*, June 24, 2020, www.nytimes.com/2020/06/24/nyregion/budget-layoffs -nyc-mta-coronavirus.html.

68 **One bar owner in Barcelona said:** *Agence France-Presse*, July 18, 2020, www .france24.com/en/20200718-barcelona-back-under-lockdown-as-virus-cases -surge.

68 **On July 23, 2020:** Andrew Van Dam, "If a business is still closed at this point in the crisis, it's probably permanent," *Washington Post*, July 23, 2020, https://www.washingtonpost.com/business/2020/07/23/permanent-business -closures-yelp/.

68 **The *New York Times* has described the impact:** Patrick McGeehan, "A Million Jobs Lost: A 'Heart Attack' for the N.Y.C. Economy," *New York Times*, July 7, 2020, https://www.nytimes.com/2020/07/07/nyregion/nyc-unemployment.html.

69 **As many as a third of the 230,000 small businesses:** "A Call for Action and Collaboration," Partnership for New York City, July 2020, https://pfnyc.org /research/a-call-for-action-and-collaboration/, 4.

70 **Since 1948, U.S. annual:** Kimberly Amadeo, "U.S. GDP by Year Compared to Recessions and Events," The Balance, March 13, 2020, www.thebalance.com /us-gdp-by-year-3305543; and "Annual Gross Domestic Product and Real GDP in the United States from 1930 to 2020," Statista, June 2, 2020, www.statista .com/statistics/1031678/gdp-and-real-gdp-united-states-1930-2019/.

71 **Its study released on June 24, 2020:** "UCLA Anderson Forecast Says U.S. Econ- omy Is in 'Depression-Like Crisis' and Will Not Return to Pre-recession Peak

Until 2023," UCLA Anderson Forecast, June 24, 2020, www.prnewswire.com
/news-releases/ucla-anderson-forecast-says-us-economy-is-in-depression-like
-crisis-and-will-not-return-to-pre-recession-peak-until-2023-301082577.html.

74 **A March 2020 study entitled**: Òscar Jordà, Sanjay R. Singh, and Alan M. Taylor, "Longer-Run Economic Consequences of Pandemics" (Federal Reserve
Bank of San Francisco Working Paper 2020-09, June 2020), www.frbsf.org
/economic-research/files/wp2020-09.pdf.

CHAPTER FOUR: DEBT AND DEFLATION DERAIL RECOVERY

75 **"Today, the United States"**: Sebastian Mallaby, "The Age of Magic Money,"
Foreign Affairs, July/August 2020, https://www.foreignaffairs.com/articles/united
-states/2020-05-29/pandemic-financial-crisis.

79 **Her views are encapsulated**: Stephanie Kelton, *The Deficit Myth: Modern
Monetary Theory and the Birth of the People's Economy* (New York: Public Affairs, 2020).

80 **Georg Friedrich Knapp**: Georg Friedrich Knapp, *The State Theory of Money*
(1924; repr., Eastford, CT: Martino Fine Books, 2013).

80 **"Only the state"**: Kelton, *Deficit Myth*, 161.

82 **"Lawmakers simply voted"**: Stephanie Kelton, "Learn to Love Trillion-Dollar
Deficits," *New York Times*, June 9, 2020, www.nytimes.com/2020/06/09/opinion
/us-deficit-coronavirus.html.

88 **This spending saturnalia includes:** Kelsey Snell, "Here's How Much Congress
Has Approved for Coronavirus Relief So Far and What It's For," NPR, May 15,
2020, www.npr.org/2020/05/15/854774681/congress-has-approved-3-trillion
-for-coronavirus-relief-so-far-heres-a-breakdown.

89 **The idea that deficit spending**: John Maynard Keynes, *The General Theory of
Employment, Interest, and Money* (1936; repr., New York: Harcourt, 1964).

92 **Of particular importance**: Carmen Reinhart and Kenneth Rogoff, "Debt and
Growth Revisited," VOX CEPR Policy Portal, August 11, 2010, https://voxeu
.org/article/debt-and-growth-revisited.

CHAPTER FIVE: CIVILIZATION'S THIN VENEER

97 **"The stranger swung"**: Katherine Anne Porter, *Collected Stories and Other
Writings* (New York: The Library of America, 2008), 282.

98 **"two living men"**: *Collected Stories and Other Writings*, 321.

100 **Still, she was almost alone:** For an extended discussion of the impact of Spanish flu on the art and literature of the time, see Laura Spinney, *Pale Rider: The
Spanish Flu of 1918 and How It Changed the World* (New York: Public Affairs,
2017), 261–71. See also Patricia Clifford, "Why Did So Few Novels Tackle the

1918 Pandemic?" *Smithsonian*, November 2017, www.smithsonianmag.com /arts-culture/flu-novels-great-pandemic-180965205/.

101 **Finally, there is a view:** Spinney, *Pale Rider*, and Catharine Arnold, *Pandemic 1918* (New York: St. Martin's Griffin, 2018).

101 **"Steinbeck's perspective was":** Arnold, *Pandemic 1918*, 13.

101 **"left a spellbinding":** Arnold, *Pandemic 1918*, 13.

102 **Barry offers excerpts:** John M. Barry, *The Great Influenza: The Story of the Deadliest Pandemic in History* (New York: Penguin, 2018), 378–88.

103 **Famed psychiatrist Karl Menninger:** Karl A. Menninger, "Influenza and Schizophrenia: An Analysis of Post-influenzal 'Dementia Precox,' as of 1918 and Five Years Later," *American Journal of Psychiatry* 5, no. 4 (April 1926): 469, https://ajp.psychiatryonline.org/doi/pdf/10.1176/ajp.82.4.469.

103 **"who caught the flu":** Spinney, *Pale Rider*, 265.

104 **"acute necrotizing hemorrhagic":** Neo Poyiadji et al., "COVID-19-Associated Acute Hemorrhagic Necrotizing Encephalopathy: CT and MRI Features," *Radiology*, March 31, 2020, https://pubs.rsna.org/doi/10.1148/radiol.2020201187.

104 **"COVID-19 can affect":** Eugene Rubin, "Effects of COVID-19 on the Brain," *Psychology Today*, April 30, 2020, www.psychologytoday.com/us/blog/demystifying -psychiatry/202004/effects-covid-19-the-brain.

105 **The Recovery Village:** Nicole LaNeve, editor, "Drug and Alcohol Use Increase During COVID-19," Recovery Village, May 29, 2020, www.therecoveryvillage .com/drug-addiction/news/drug-alcohol-use-rising-during-covid/.

105 **"COVID-19 along with":** Sarah L. Hagerty and Leanne M. Williams, "The Impact of COVID-19 on Mental Health: The Interactive Roles of Brain Biotypes and Human Connection," *Brain, Behavior, & Immunity—Health* 5 (May 2020), www.ncbi.nlm.nih.gov/pmc/articles/PMC7204757/.

106 **"Nationwide, mental health":** Christine Vestal, "Fear, Isolation, Depression: The Mental Health Fallout of a Worldwide Pandemic," Stateline, Pew Charitable Trusts, May 12, 2020, www.pewtrusts.org/en/research-and-analysis/blogs /stateline/2020/05/12/fear-isolation-depression-the-mental-health-fallout -of-a-worldwide-pandemic.

107 **A growing body of research:** For a good overview of research in the area of the neurological impact of SARS-CoV-2, see Megan Molteni, "What Does Covid-19 Do to Your Brain?" *Wired*, April 15, 2020, www.wired.com/story/what-does -covid-19-do-to-your-brain/.

112 **Reuters reported that Arkansas:** Raphael Satter, "To Keep COVID-19 Patients Home, Some U.S. States Weigh House Arrest Tech," *Reuters*, May 7, 2020, www.reuters.com/article/us-health-coronavirus-quarantine-tech/to -keep-covid-19-patients-home-some-u-s-states-weigh-house-arrest-tech -idUSKBN22J1U8.

112 **Eminent historian Victor Davis Hanson:** Victor Davis Hanson, "Not-So-

Retiring Retired Military Leaders," *National Review*, June 7, 2020, www.nation
alreview.com/2020/06/not-so-retiring-retired-military-leaders/.

114 **Antifa was long waiting:** Bill Gertz, "Antifa Planned Anti-government Insurgency for Months, Law Enforcement Official Says," *Washington Times*, June 3,
2020, www.washingtontimes.com/news/2020/jun/3/antifa-planned-anti-govern
ment-insurgency-george-f/.

114 ***Wall Street Journal* deputy editor Daniel Henninger:** Daniel Henninger,
"Progressives to Cities: Drop Dead," *Wall Street Journal*, July 22, 2020, www.wsj
.com/articles/progressives-to-cities-drop-dead-11595458490.

115 **"The economic repercussions":** Branko Milanović, "The Real Pandemic Danger Is Social Collapse," *Foreign Affairs*, March 19, 2020, www.foreignaffairs
.com/print/node/1125708.

116 **"It may be difficult":** James Rickards, *Aftermath: Seven Secrets of Wealth Preservation in the Coming Chaos* (New York: Portfolio, 2019), 289–91.

CHAPTER SIX: INVESTING IN A POST-PANDEMIC WORLD

119 **"The most extraordinary thing":** H. G. Wells, *The War of the Worlds* (1898;
repr., New York: Signet Classics, 2007), 38.

120 **"And scattered about it":** Wells, *War of the Worlds*, 184–85.

122 **"It was basically free":** Gregory Zuckerman and Mischa Frankl-Duval,
"Individuals Roll the Dice on Stocks as Veterans Fret," *Wall Street Journal*, June 9,
2020, www.wsj.com/articles/individuals-roll-the-dice-on-stocks-as-veterans-fret
-11591732784.

132 **It's interesting to hear analysts:** See Graham Allison, *Destined for War: Can
America and China Escape Thucydides's Trap?* (Boston: Mariner Books, 2018).

145 **"Social and economic landscapes":** Priscilla DeGregory, "Valentino Sues NYC
Landlord to Get Out of 5th Ave Lease Amid Pandemic," *New York Post*, June 22,
2020, https://nypost.com/2020/06/22/valentino-sues-nyc-landlord-to-get-out-of
-5th-ave-lease/.

CONCLUSION

153 **"Government cannot restore"** : Victor Davis Hanson, "Losing Our Fears, in
War and Plague," Townhall, May 14, 2020, https://townhall.com/columnists
/victordavishanson/2020/05/14/losing-our-fears-in-war-and-plague-n2568733.

158 **"One morning, FDR":** Amity Shlaes, *The Forgotten Man: A New History of the
Great Depression* (New York: Harper Perennial, 2008), 148.

SELECTED SOURCES

ARTICLES

Amadeo, Kimberly. "U.S. GDP by Year Compared to Recessions and Events," The Balance, March 13, 2020.

Andersen, Kristian G., et al. "The Proximal Origin of SARS-CoV-2." *Nature Medicine* 26 (April 2020): 450–52.

Anderson, Roy M., et al. "How Will Country-Based Mitigation Measures Influence the Course of the COVID-19 Epidemic?" *The Lancet* 395, no. 10228 (March 21–27, 2020): 395.

Begley, Sharon. "New Analysis Recommends Less Reliance on Ventilators to Treat Coronavirus Patients." STAT, April 21, 2020.

Bell, Stephanie. "The Role of the State and the Hierarchy of Money." *Cambridge Journal of Economics* 25, no. 2 (March 2001): 149–63.

Ben-Israel, Isaac. "The End of Exponential Growth: The Decline in the Spread of Coronavirus." *Times of Israel*, April 19, 2020.

Branswell, Helen. "Why 'Flattening the Curve' May Be the World's Best Bet to Slow the Coronavirus." STAT, March 11, 2020.

Brown, Lee. "Wuhan Lab Admits to Having Three Live Strains of Bat Coronavirus on Site." *New York Post*, May 24, 2020.

Butler, Declan. "Engineered Bat Virus Stirs Debate over Risky Research." *Nature*, November 12, 2015.

Centers for Disease Control and Prevention. "Frequently Asked Questions: Pandemic Flu and the Updated Community Mitigation Guidelines," August 3, 2017.

Centers for Disease Control and Prevention. "Interim Pre-pandemic Planning Guidance: Community Strategy for Pandemic Influenza Mitigation in the United

States—Early, Targeted, Layered Use of Nonpharmaceutical Interventions," February 2007.

Chan, Minnie, and William Zheng. "Meet the Major General on China's Coronavirus Scientific Front Line." *South China Morning Post*, March 3, 2020.

Chen, Sharon, Claire Che, and Jason Gale. "China's New Outbreak Shows Signs the Virus Could Be Changing." Bloomberg News, May 20, 2020.

Clifford, Patricia. "Why Did So Few Novels Tackle the 1918 Pandemic?" *Smithsonian*, November 2017.

Condon, Bernard, Jennifer Peltz, and Jim Mustian. "AP Count: Over 4,500 Virus Patients Sent to NY Nursing Homes." ABC News, May 22, 2020.

Corcoran, Kiernan. "An Infamous WHO Tweet Saying There Was 'No Clear Evidence' COVID-19 Could Spread Between Humans Was Posted for 'Balance' to Reflect Findings from China." Business Insider, April 18, 2020.

"Coronavirus: Prof. Neil Ferguson Quits Government Role after 'Undermining' Lockdown." BBC News, May 6, 2020.

"Coronavirus: US to Halt Funding to WHO, Says Trump." BBC News, April 15, 2020.

Cotton, Tom. "Coronavirus and the Laboratories in Wuhan." *Wall Street Journal*, April 21, 2020.

Davis, William. "How China's Coronavirus Cover-up Happened." Daily Caller, April 19, 2020.

Dondorp, Arjen N., et al. "Respiratory Support in Novel Coronavirus Disease (COVID-19) Patients, with a Focus on Resource-Limited Settings." *American Society of Tropical Medicine and Hygiene* 102, no. 6 (June 2, 2020): 1191–97.

du Toit, Pieter. "Inside SA's Frightening Covid-19 Projections and Why Transparency Is Important." news24, May 20, 2020.

El-Erian, Mohamed A. "Wall Street Is Flourishing While Main Street Is Suffering." *Foreign Policy*, May 29, 2020.

Ernst, Douglas. "Coronavirus USA: States Explore House Arrest Technology to Enforce Quarantines." *Washington Times*, May 7, 2020.

Fink, Sheri. "Hospitals Move into Next Phase as New York Passes Viral Peak." *New York Times*, May 20, 2020.

Gertz, Bill. "Antifa Planned Anti-government Insurgency for Months, Law Enforcement Official Says." *Washington Times*, June 3, 2020.

Gertz, Bill. "Coronavirus Origins in Lab Not Ruled Out by Scientific Studies." *Washington Times*, April 21, 2020.

Gertz, Bill. "Wuhan Lab 'Most Likely' Coronavirus Source, U.S. Government Analysis Finds." *Washington Times*, April 28, 2020.

Glass, Robert J., et al. "Targeted Social Distancing Designs for Pandemic Influenza." *Emerging Infectious Diseases Journal* 12, no. 11 (November 2006): 1671–81.

Hagemann, Hannah. "U.K.'s Boris Johnson Says His Battle with Coronavirus 'Could Have Gone Either Way.'" NPR, May 3, 2020.

Hagerty, Sarah L., and Leanne M. Williams. "The Impact of COVID-19 on Mental

Health: The Interactive Roles of Brain Biotypes and Human Connection." *Brain, Behavior, & Immunity—Health* 5, May 2020.

Hanson, Victor Davis. "Losing Our Fears, in War and Plague." Townhall, May 14, 2020.

Hanson, Victor Davis. "Not-So-Retiring Retired Military Leaders." *National Review*, June 7, 2020.

Hegarty, Stephanie. "The Chinese Doctor Who Tried to Warn Others About Coronavirus." BBC News, February 6, 2020.

Horowitz, Daniel. "The CDC Confirms Remarkable Low Coronavirus Death Rate. Where Is the Media?" Conservative Review, May 22, 2020.

House Foreign Affairs Committee Minority Staff Interim Report. "The Origins of the COVID-19 Global Pandemic, Including the Roles of the Chinese Communist Party and the World Health Organization," June 12, 2020.

Howell, Tom, and Dave Boyer. "Trump Pulls U.S. Out of World Health Organization, Slaps Penalties on China over Hong Kong Action." *Washington Times*, May 29, 2020.

Huang, Chaolin, et al. "Clinical Features of Patients Infected with 2019 Novel Coronavirus in Wuhan, China." *The Lancet* 395, no. 10223 (January 24, 2020): 497–506.

Ignatius, David. "How Did Covid-19 Begin? Its Initial Origin Story Is Shaky." *Washington Post*, April 2, 2020.

Inglesby, Thomas V., et al. "Disease Mitigation Measures in the Control of Pandemic Influenza." *Biosecurity and Bioterrorism: Biodefense Strategy, Practice, and Science* 4, no. 4 (2006).

Kahn, Jo. "We've Never Made a Successful Vaccine for a Coronavirus Before. This Is Why It's So Difficult." ABC News, April 16, 2020.

Kelton, Stephanie. "Why I'm Not Worried About America's Trillion-Dollar Deficits." *New York Times*, June 9, 2020.

Korber, B., et al. "Spike Mutation Pipeline Reveals the Emergence of a More Transmissible Form of SARS-CoV-2." bioRxiv, April 30, 2020.

Krugman, Paul. "How Many Will Die for the Dow?" *New York Times*, May 21, 2020.

LaNeve, Nicole, ed. "Drug and Alcohol Use Increase During COVID-19." Recovery Village, May 29, 2020.

Li, Wei, et al., "High Potency of a Bivalent Human V_H Domain in SARS-CoV-1 Animal Models." (Journal Pre-Proof) *Cell*, September 4, 2020.

Liping, Gu. "Official: Wuhan Seafood Market May Be the Victim of Coronavirus." Ecns.com, May 26, 2020.

Lipton, Eric, and Jennifer Steinhauer. "The Untold Story of the Birth of Social Distancing." *New York Times*, April 22, 2020.

Ma, Josephine. "Coronavirus: China's First Confirmed Covid-19 Case Traced Back to November 17." *South China Morning Post*, March 13, 2020.

Markson, Sharri. "Coronavirus May Have Been a 'Cell-Culture Experiment' Gone Wrong." Sky News, May 24, 2020.

Markson, Sharri. "Coronavirus NSW: Dossier Lays Out Case Against China Bat Virus Program." *Daily Telegraph*, May 3, 2020.

McKay, Betsey, and Daniela Hernandez. "Coronavirus Hijacks the Body from Head to Toe, Perplexing Doctors." *Wall Street Journal*, May 7, 2020.

Medvin, Marina. "Israeli Professor Shows Virus Follows Fixed Pattern." Townhall, April 15, 2020.

Menninger, Karl A. "Influenza and Schizophrenia: An Analysis of Post-influenzal 'Dementia Precox,' as of 1918 and Five Years Later." *American Journal of Psychiatry* 5, no. 4, (April 1926): 469–529.

Milanović, Branko. "The Real Pandemic Danger Is Social Collapse." *Foreign Affairs*, March 19, 2020.

Miller, Andrew Mark. "California Doctors Say They've Seen More Deaths from Suicide Than Coronavirus Since Lockdowns." *Washington Examiner*, May 21, 2020.

Miller, Hannah, and Christina Cheddar Berk. "JC Penney Could Join a Growing List of Bankruptcies During the Coronavirus Pandemic." CNBC, May 15, 2020.

Molteni, Megan. "What Does Covid-19 Do to Your Brain?" *Wired*, April 15, 2020.

Moore, Kristine A., et al. "The Future of the COVID-19 Pandemic: Lessons Learned from Pandemic Influenza." Center for Infectious Disease Research and Policy, University of Minnesota, April 30, 2020.

New York State Department of Health. "Advisory: Hospital Discharges and Admissions to Nursing Homes," March 25, 2020.

New York State Department of Health. "Advisory: Hospital Discharges and Admissions to ACFs," April 7, 2020.

Nikel, David. "Norway Scientist Claims Report Proves Coronavirus Was Lab-Made." *Forbes*, June 7, 2020.

"Open Letter From Medical Doctors and Health Professionals to All Belgian Authorities and All Belgian Media." American Institute for Economic Research, September 20, 2020.

Poyiadji, Neo, et al. "COVID-19-Associated Acute Hemorrhagic Necrotizing Encephalopathy: CT and MRI Features." *Radiology*, March 31, 2020.

Qualls, Noreen, et al. "Community Mitigation Guidelines to Prevent Pandemic Influenza—United States, 2017." *Morbidity and Mortality Weekly Report* 66, no. 1 (April 21, 2017).

Redford, Audrey, and Thomas K. Duncan. "Drugs, Suicide and Crime: Empirical Estimates of the Human Toll of the Shutdown." American Institute for Economic Research, March 28, 2020.

Reinhart, Carmen, and Kenneth Rogoff. "Debt and Growth Revisited." VOX CEPR Policy Portal, August 11, 2010.

Reitz, Michael J. "What's Wrong with Gov. Whitmer's Stay-at-Home Order." Mackinac Center for Public Policy, April 15, 2020.

Rettner, Rachael. "Coronavirus Outbreak Is 'Public Health Emergency of International Concern,' WHO Declares." Live Science, January 30, 2020.

Rettner, Rachael. "Up to 25% of People with COVID-19 May Not Show Symptoms." Live Science, April 1, 2020.

Rogin, Josh. "State Department Cables Warned of Safety Issues at Wuhan Lab Studying Bat Coronaviruses." *Washington Post*, April 14, 2020.

Rubin, Eugene. "Effects of COVID-19 on the Brain." *Psychology Today*, April 30, 2020.

Scissors, Derek. "Estimating the True Number of China's COVID-19 Cases." American Enterprise Institute, April 2020.

Sherfinski, David, and Stephan Dinan. "Unemployment More Lucrative Than Work for Most Would-Be Recipients in Extension: CBO." *Washington Times*, June 4, 2020.

Sino Biological. "Hong Kong Flu (1968 Influenza Pandemic)." No date.

Snell, Kelsey. "Here's How Much Congress Has Approved for Coronavirus Relief So Far and What It's For." NPR, May 15, 2020.

Sørensen, B., A. Susrud, and A. G. Dalgleish. "Biovacc-19: A Candidate Vaccine for Covid-19 (SARS-CoV-2) Developed from Analysis of Its General Method of Action for Infectivity." *Quarterly Review of Biophysics*, May 28, 2020.

Spitznagel, Eric. "Why American Life Went On as Normal During the Killer Pandemic of 1969." *New York Post*, May 16, 2020.

"U.S. Entered a Recession in February: Live Updates." *New York Times*, June 8, 2020.

Vartabedian, Ralph. "Scientists Say a Now-Dominant Strain of the Coronavirus Appears to Be More Contagious Than Original." *Los Angeles Times*, May 5, 2020.

Vestal, Christine. "Fear, Isolation, Depression: The Mental Health Fallout of a Worldwide Pandemic." Stateline, Pew Charitable Trusts, May 12, 2020.

Watson, Steve. "US Intel Officials Believe 45,000 Corpses Were Incinerated in One Fortnight in Wuhan." Summit News, April 28, 2020.

Webster, Robert G. "Wet Markets—a Continuing Source of Severe Acute Respiratory Syndrome and Influenza?" *The Lancet* 363, no. 9404 (January 17, 2004): 234–36.

"What Do You Like Most About Working from Home?" Pioneer Institute, June 11, 2020.

Yan, Li-Meng, et al., "Unusual Features of the SARS-CoV-2 Genome Suggesting Sophisticated Laboratory Modification Rather Than Natural Evolution and Delineation of Its Probable Synthetic Route," Rule of Law Society & Rule of Law Foundation, *Zenodo*, September 14, 2020.

Ying, Fu. "Shape Global Narratives for Telling China's Stories." *China Daily*, April 4, 2020.

Zehngli-Li, Shi, et al. "A SARS-like Cluster of Circulating Bat Coronaviruses Shows Potential for Human Emergence." *Nature Medicine*, November 9, 2015.

Zuckerman, Gregory, and Mischa Frankl-Duval. "Individuals Roll the Dice on Stocks as Veterans Fret." *Wall Street Journal*, June 9, 2020.

BOOKS

Allison, Graham. *Destined for War: Can America and China Escape Thucydides's Trap?* Boston: Mariner Books, 2018.

Arnold, Catharine. *Pandemic 1918*. New York: St. Martin's Griffin, 2018.

Barry, John M. *The Great Influenza: The Story of the Deadliest Pandemic in History.* New York: Penguin Books, 2018.

Berenson, Alex. *Unreported Truths About COVID-19 and Lockdowns.* New Providence: Bowker, 2020. Part 1, "Introduction and Death Counts and Estimates."

Boccaccio, Giovanni. *The Decameron.* 14th century. Reprint, New York: W. W. Norton, 2013.

Camus, Albert. *The Plague.* 1947. Reprint, New York: Vintage International, 1991.

Crosby, Alfred W. *America's Forgotten Pandemic.* New York: Cambridge University Press, 2010.

Davies, Pete. *The Devil's Flu: The World's Deadliest Influenza Epidemic and the Scientific Hunt for the Virus That Caused It.* New York: Henry Holt, 2000.

Fang, Fang. *Wuhan Diary.* New York: HarperCollins, 2020.

Garrett, Garet. *A Bubble That Broke the World.* Boston: Little, Brown, 1932.

Gertz, Bill. *How China's Communist Party Made the World Sick.* New York: Encounter Books, 2020.

Grant, James. *The Forgotten Depression: 1921: The Crash That Cured Itself.* New York: Simon & Shuster, 2014.

Kelton, Stephanie. *The Deficit Myth: Modern Monetary Theory and the Birth of the People's Economy.* New York: Public Affairs, 2020.

Keynes, John Maynard. *The General Theory of Employment, Interest, and Money.* New York: Harcourt, 1964.

Knapp, Georg Friedrich. *The State Theory of Money.* Eastford, CT: Martino Fine Books, 2013.

Porter, Katherine Anne. *Collected Stories and Other Writings.* New York: Library of America, 2008.

Preston, Richard. *The Demon in the Freezer.* New York: Random House, 2002.

Rappleye, Charles. *Herbert Hoover in the White House: The Ordeal of the Presidency.* New York: Simon & Schuster, 2016.

Reinhart, Carmen M., and Kenneth S. Rogoff. *This Time Is Different: Eight Centuries of Financial Folly.* Princeton, NJ: Princeton University Press, 2009.

Rickards, James. *Aftermath: Seven Secrets of Wealth Preservation in the Coming Chaos.* New York: Portfolio, 2019.

Shlaes, Amity. *Coolidge.* New York: HarperCollins, 2013.

Shlaes, Amity. *The Forgotten Man: A New History of the Great Depression.* New York: Harper Perennial, 2008.

Spinney, Laura. *Pale Rider: The Spanish Flu of 1918 and How It Changed the World.* New York: Public Affairs, 2017.

Taylor, Frederick. *The Downfall of Money: Germany's Hyperinflation and the Destruction of the Middle Class.* New York: Bloomsbury, 2013.

Wells, H. G. *The War of the Worlds.* 1898. Reprint, New York: Signet Classics, 2007.